CHICKEN SOUP
FOR THE SOUL
NASCAR XTREME
RACE JOURNAL
FOR KIDS

Jack Canfield
Mark Victor Hansen
Matthew E. Adams

Health Communications, Inc.
Deerfield Beach, Florida

www.hcibooks.com
www.chickensoup.com

Library of Congress Cataloging-in-Publication Data
is available from the Library of Congress.

©2005 Jack Canfield and Mark Victor Hansen
ISBN 0-7573-0283-1

Publisher: Health Communications, Inc.
            3201 S.W. 15th Street
            Deerfield Beach, FL 33442–8190

Cover design by Andrea Perrine Brower
Inside book design by Lawna Patterson Oldfield
All photos ©NASCAR Photography/Sherryl Creekmore

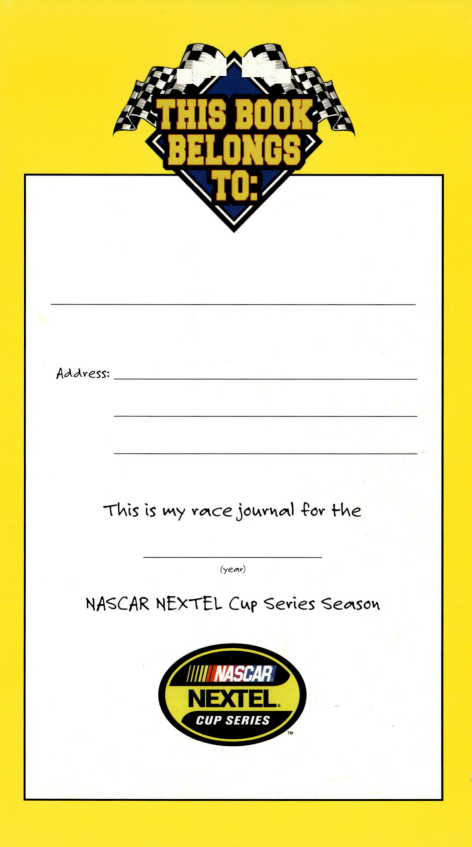

THIS BOOK BELONGS TO:

Address: _____

_____

_____

This is my race journal for the

_____

(year)

NASCAR NEXTEL Cup Series Season

CONTENTS

LET'S GO RACIN'

NASCAR *memories last forever.*

My first NASCAR memory is . . .

My first NASCAR memories were when my mom used to force my sister to turn off her music videos so Mom could watch the end of the race. My sister would sit on the coach and sulk, telling Mom that NASCAR was " a dumb sport, all they do is go around and round."
Today, my sister is the biggest NASCAR fan I know. I guess Mom really does know best—LOL!!!!

Ashley

My first NASCAR memory is when my grandfather would bounce me on his knee while he made engine nois and did the play-by-play about who we were passing and leaving the dust. We must have won the Daytona 500 at least a thousand times!

Pat

My first memory of NASCAR was when I was seven and I went over to my grandpa's house to get an ice cream. He had NASCAR poster: and stickers all over every wall and he was watching a race. I'll never forget how he was screaming at the TV like the drivers could actually hear him!

Sissy

My first NASCAR memory is . . .

_____

_____

_____

_____

_____

_____

_____

"Stock car racing
is the most exciting sport
in the world."

—RICHARD PETTY

NASCAR is the most heart pounding, hands sweating, ears aching, stomach churning, non-stop action you will find anywhere on the earth. If you have never been to a **NASCAR** race, all it will take is one and you will be hooked for life. If you go to races regularly, you already know what it is like to feel a wave of excitement sweep through one hundred thousand people as a massive wall of sound roars down the straight-away. You have felt the unbridled power of almost 800 horsepower raise you up from your seat and make you feel as if you are about to be swept away by forty-three of the fastest and most beautiful race cars you have ever seen, whizzing by you in a blinding parade of color and spectacle.

What is **NASCAR**? It is simply the greatest sport, period. It combines technology, science, math, teamwork, strategy, hard work, discipline, planning, dedication, faith and luck. The challenges, excitement, adversity and triumph in **NASCAR** are a reflection of life and we hope that as you enjoy the races you also learn something about yourself.

The *NASCAR Xtreme Race Journal for Kids* gives you all the information you could ever need to fully enjoy following **NASCAR**. Each of the following chapters concentrates on a particular track providing you with tons of facts including location, Web site, seating capacity, track shape, and race records. You'll have hours of fun trying to figure out the answers to the ultimate trivia questions and word finds. Finally, each chapter has all the space you need to literally become a part of this book, by writing in your own journal entries for each race of the season. This journal will become your permanent record of your favorite drivers and **NASCAR** races.

THE CAR

❶ **FRONT GRILL OPENINGS:** Allow air to pass through the radiator and ensure that the engine performs at the optimum temperature.

❷ **HOOD PINS:** Four metal-and-wire pins with wire tethers that keep the hood closed.

③ SHOCK ABSORBERS: Help control the compression and rebound of the suspension springs and provide a smooth and controlled ride to the driver.

④ JACK POST: This is the area where the jackman must place the jack on each side of the car during a pit stop.

⑤ ROLL CAGE: A cage made of steel tubing inside the car that protects the driver from impacts and rollovers.

⑥ WINDOW NET: Safety device located on the driver's side window that helps keep his or her head and arms inside the car during an accident.

⑦ TELEVISION CAMERA: Allows *NASCAR* fans a great view of their favorite drivers in race traffic.

⑧ ROOF STRIPS: Two half-inch-tall aluminum strips that run lengthwise on the roof and help stop the car from turning over when it is turned sideways during a spin or accident.

⑨ ROOF FLAPS: Help stop the car from becoming airborne when it is turned sideways or backward during a spin or accident.

⑩ JACKING BOLT: Area where the crew uses a tool to adjust the handling of the car by altering pressure on the rear springs.

⑪ REAR SPOILER: Deflects the air coming off the roof and onto the rear deck lid, which in turn creates greater downforce and more traction for the rear wheels.

⑫ FUEL CELL: Holding tank for car's gasoline. It can hold 22 gallons of fuel.

⑬ DECK LID: Slang term for the trunk lid of a stock car.

⑭ FIREWALL: Steel plate that separates the engine compartment from the driver's compartment of the car. Also used at the rear to separate the fuel cell compartment from the driver's compartment.

⑮ TRACK BAR: Lateral bar that keeps the rear tires centered within the body of the car.

⑯ SWAY OR ANTI-ROLL BAR: Used to resist or counteract the rolling force of the car body through the turns.

⑰ ALTERNATE EXIT: More commonly known as a "roof hatch," it provides drivers with an alternate exit from the car in the event of an emergency situation.

THE COCKPIT

The cockpit of a stock car serves as the "weekend office" for the drivers. Each team configures the cockpit differently; there is an extensive array of safety features, as well as instrument gauges that help the driver monitor the car's performance.

❶ MAIN SWITCH PANEL: Contains switches for starter, ignition, and cooling fans

❷ TACHOMETER: Monitors revolutions per minute (RPMs) of engine, assisting driver in selecting gears and monitoring engine power

❸ ENGINE GAUGE CLUSTER: Monitors engine oil pressure, water temperature, oil temperature, voltage and fuel pressure

❹ AUXILIARY SWITCHES: Can serve a number of purposes, including turning on the backup ignition system, ventilating fans, or helmet cooling system.

❺ MASTER SWITCH: Shuts down electrical system in emergency situations

❻ IGNITION KILL SWITCH: Shuts off engine in emergency situations

7 **RADIO BUTTON:** Controls communication to pits and race spotter

8 **GEARSHIFT:** Controls four-speed manual transmission

9 **SAFETY SEAT:** Provides extra support and protection for head, shoulders, ribs and lower extremities

10 **HEAD AND NECK RESTRAINT:** *NASCAR* mandates the use of a head-and-neck restraint system, either the approved HANS Device or Hutchens Device.

11 **WINDOW NET:** Helps keep driver's arm inside the car during accidents

12 **REAR VIEW MIRROR**

13 **FRESH AIR VENT:** Directs outside air into the driving compartment

14 **MAIN REAR VIEW MIRROR**

15 **FIRE EXTINGUISHER**

16 **SEAT BELT HARNESS**

17 **FIRE EXTINGUISHER SWITCH:** Discharges fire-suppressing chemicals into the driving compartment

18 **FIRE EXTINGUISHER DISCHARGE NOZZLE**

19 **HELMET HOOK**

THE PIT STOP

Per *NASCAR* rules, seven crew members are routinely allowed over the wall during pit stops. At times, *NASCAR* will inform teams that an eighth crew member will be allowed over the wall to clean the windshield.

An average efficient pit stop that consists of the changing of all four tires and a full tank of fuel can take anywhere between 13 and 15 seconds. The amount of pit stops during a race change due to numerous factors—race length, caution flags, fuel mileage, tire wear and pit strategy are a few. Here's a look at the pit crew and their responsibilities during a routine stop during a race.

1 **REAR TIRE CARRIER:** Assists the rear tire changer by handing him a new, right-side tire he has carried from behind the pit wall. May also adjust the rear jack bolt to change the car's handling.

2 **JACKMAN:** Operates a 20 pound hydraulic jack that is used to raise the car for tire changes. After new tires are bolted onto the right side of the car, he drops the car to the ground and repeats the process on the left side.

❸ REAR TIRE CHANGER: First removes and replaces right rear tire using an air-powered impact wrench to loosen and tighten five lug nuts holding the tire rim in place. He then moves to the opposite side of the car to change the left rear tire.

❹ FRONT TIRE CARRIER: Assists the front tire changer by handing him a new, right-side tire that he has carried from behind the pit wall. He repeats the process on the left side of the car with a tire rolled to him by another crew member from behind the pit wall.

❺ FRONT TIRE CHANGER: First removes and replaces right front tire using an air-powered impact wrench to loosen and tighten five lug nuts holding the tire rim in place. He then moves to the opposite side of the car to change the left front tire.

❻ CATCH CAN MAN: Holds a can that collects overflow from the fuel cell as it is being filled. He also signals the rest of the team that the refueling process is finished by raising his hand.

❼ GAS MAN: Empties two 12-gallon *(81 pounds each)* dump-cans of fuel into the car's 22 gallon fuel cell.

⑧ SUPPORT CREW: Assists the "over the wall" crew by rolling them tires, handing them fuel, and retrieving air hoses and wrenches. According to NASCAR rules, support crew members must remain behind the pit wall during all stops.

⑨ EXTRA MAN: On occasion, and at the discretion of NASCAR officials, an eighth or "extra man" is allowed over the wall to clean the windshield and assist the driver, if necessary.

⑩ CREW CHIEF: On top of the team's "war wagon," there are other crew members who monitor the team's position in the race along with the crew chief (standing), who oversees the crew and can give commands to them via radio, if needed.

⑪ NASCAR OFFICIAL: Watches for rules violations and helps maintain pit lane safety.

DRAFTING

AERODYNAMICS: The study of how the airflow affects a stock car while racing.

DRAG: The resistance a car experiences when passing through air at high speeds.

DOWNFORCE: Downforce can be changed to make the car's grip or traction on the track better. One way this can be done is by adjusting the spoiler on the car. As downforce is increased, the grip/traction is increased as well as tire wear. Increasing downforce creates more drag on the car, which reduces fuel efficiency.

DRAFT: The aerodynamic effect that lets two or more cars traveling nose to tail to run faster than a single car. When one car follows another closely, the one in front punches through the air and gives a cleaner, less resistant path for the cars behind it.

DRAFTING: The practice of two or more cars running nose to tail to create more speed for the group. The lead car displaces the air in front of it, creates a vacuum effect between its rear end and the nose of the second car and pulls the trailing cars along with it with less overall resistance. Two or more cars drafting will travel faster than a single car.

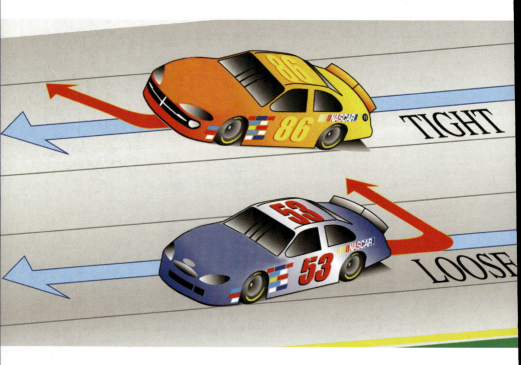

TIGHT: Also known as understeer. This happens when the front wheels lose traction before the rear wheels. The stock car has trouble steering sharply and smoothly through the turns as the front end pushes toward the wall.

LOOSE: Also known as oversteer. This happens when the rear tires of the stock car have trouble sticking in the corners. This makes the car "fishtail" as the rear end swings outward while turning in the corners.

THE TRACKS

There are four different types of tracks:

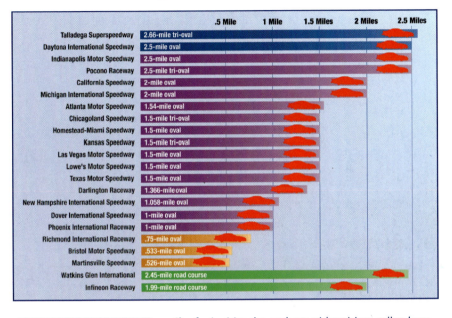

	.5 Mile	1 Mile	1.5 Miles	2 Miles	2.5 Miles
Talladega Superspeedway	2.66-mile tri-oval				
Daytona International Speedway	2.5-mile oval				
Indianapolis Motor Speedway	2.5-mile oval				
Pocono Raceway	2.5-mile tri-oval				
California Speedway	2-mile oval				
Michigan International Speedway	2-mile oval				
Atlanta Motor Speedway	1.54-mile oval				
Chicagoland Speedway	1.5-mile tri-oval				
Homestead-Miami Speedway	1.5-mile oval				
Kansas Speedway	1.5-mile tri-oval				
Las Vegas Motor Speedway	1.5-mile oval				
Lowe's Motor Speedway	1.5-mile oval				
Texas Motor Speedway	1.5-mile oval				
Darlington Raceway	1.366-mile oval				
New Hampshire International Speedway	1.058-mile oval				
Dover International Speedway	1-mile oval				
Phoenix International Raceway	1-mile oval				
Richmond International Raceway	.75-mile oval				
Bristol Motor Speedway	.533-mile oval				
Martinsville Speedway	.526-mile oval				
Watkins Glen International	2.45-mile road course				
Infineon Raceway	1.99-mile road course				

SUPERSPEEDWAYS are the fastest tracks and are at least two miles long and provide some of the greatest thrills in *NASCAR* as drivers push their cars close to 200 mph while just inches apart from their competitors.

SPEEDWAYS are oval-shaped tracks between one mile and two miles. Although many tracks fit this description, each track has a unique configuration. The bank of the turns can range from nine degrees to twenty-five degrees. The actual racing surface can be asphalt or concrete.

SHORT TRACKS are less than one mile long. When watching a short track race, watch for bumping and banging between the competitors. With little room to move around, short track races are the most action-packed in *NASCAR*.

ROAD COURSES differ from any other type of track, as they do not take the traditional oval shape. Drivers have to maneuver their cars over a complex arrangement of left and right turns, most of the turns at different angles.

TRACK FACTS

LONGEST TRACK: Talladega Superspeedway—Talladega, Alabama
2.66–mile oval

SHORTEST TRACK: Martinsville Speedway—Martinsville, Virginia
.526-mile oval

LONGEST FRONTSTRETCH: Talladega Superspeedway—Talladega, Alabama
4,300 feet

SHORTEST FRONTSTRETCH: Bristol Motor Speedway—Bristol, Tennessee
650 feet

MOST BANKING: Bristol Motor Speedway—Bristol, Tennessee
36 degrees

LEAST BANKING: Indianapolis Motor Speedway—Indianapolis, Indiana
9 degrees

FASTEST RACE (AVERAGE SPEED): Talladega Superspeedway
188.354 mph (Mark Martin—May 10, 1997)

LEAST-FAST RACE (AVERAGE SPEED): Martinsville Speedway
67.658 mph (Jeff Gordon—Oct. 19, 2003)

NASCAR TERMS

BANKING: The sloping of a racetrack, particularly at a curve or corner, from the apron to the outside wall. Degree of banking refers to the height of a track's slope at its outside edge.

CHASSIS: The steel structure or frame of the car.

FUEL CELL: A holding tank for a race car's supply of gasoline. It holds approximately twenty-two gallons.

MARBLES: Excess rubber build-up above the upper groove on the racetrack.

PIT ROAD: The area where pit crews service the cars. Generally located along the front straightaway, but because of space limitations, some tracks sport pit roads on both the front and back straightaways.

PIT STALL: The area along pit road that is designated for a particular team's use during pit stops.

POLE POSITION: Term for the first position on the starting grid, awarded to the fastest qualifier.

RESTRICTOR PLATE: A thin metal plate with four holes that restrict airflow from the carburetor into the engine. Used to reduce horsepower and keep speeds down. The restrictor plates are currently used at Daytona International Speedway and Talladega Superspeedway, the two biggest and fastest tracks in *NASCAR*.

SPLASH AND GO: A quick pit stop that involves nothing more than refueling the race car with the amount of fuel necessary to finish the race.

STOP AND GO: A penalty, usually assessed for speeding on pit road or for unsafe driving. The car must be brought onto pit road at the appropriate speed and stopped for one full second in the team's pit stall before returning to the track.

TEMPLATE: A device used to check the body shape and size, to ensure compliance with the rules. The template closely resembles the shape of the factory version of the car.

NASCAR TRIVIA

1. *NASCAR* was founded in:
- **A** 1964
- **B** 1947
- **C** 1971
- **D** 1935

2. The *NASCAR NEXTEL* Cup Series consists of:
- **A** 100 Races
- **B** 25 Races
- **C** 47 Races
- **D** 36 Races

3. The *NASCAR NEXTEL* Cup Series is completed over how many tracks?
- **A** 36 Tracks
- **B** 23 Tracks
- **C** 14 Tracks
- **D** 42 Tracks

4. The *NASCAR NEXTEL* Cup Series travels to how many states each year?
- **A** 50 States
- **B** 43 States
- **C** 23 States
- **D** 19 States

5. *NASCAR*, through all of its series, has how many events each year?
- **A** 200
- **B** 414
- **C** 1,800
- **D** 1,092

6. How many tracks do all of these events take place on?
- **A** 1,092
- **B** 845
- **C** 180
- **D** 110

7. *NASCAR* is second highest-rated televised sport in the United States. What sport is first?
- **A** Golf
- **B** Football
- **C** Baseball
- **D** Basketball

8. How many people attend all of *NASCAR'S* top three series combined?
- **A** 5 Million
- **B** 500,000
- **C** 13 Million
- **D** 1.2 Million

9. Overall, *NASCAR* has how many fans?
- **A** 5 Million
- **B** 500,000
- **C** 75 Million
- **D** 1 Billion

10. The Chairman of the board and Chief Executive officer of *NASCAR* is?
- **A** Brian Z. France
- **B** Matthew E. Adams
- **C** Thomas Pickett
- **D** Chris Kersten

MY FAVORITE DRIVER

Name: _____

Birthdate: _____ Height: _____ Weight: _____ lbs.

Color Eyes: _____ Color Hair: _____

Car #: _____ Model: _____

Sponsors: _____

_____

Owner: _____ Crew Chief: _____

Teammates:

_____, Car #_____   _____, Car #_____

_____, Car #_____   _____, Car #_____

_____, Car #_____   _____, Car #_____

First Year in **NASCAR NEXTEL** Cup: _____

First Race Won: Track _____ Date _____

Number of Career Victories: ___ Top Five Finishes: ___ Top Ten Finishes: ___

His favorite track: _____

He's my favorite driver because: _____

_____

_____

The best thing about him is: _____

_____

_____

If I met him, the first thing I'd ask would be: _____

_____

_____

My Favorite Driver is:

My favorite driver is Jeff Gordon because when I was a little kid I used to run around all the time and my Dad used to tell me that I was "as fast as Jeff Gordon."

—Jamie

I met Michael Waltrip at an autograph session. We only had a few moments to talk, but when I told him that I wanted to be a racecar driver, he told me that I can do anything I put my mind to. He is my hero!

—Stacy

Kyle Petty will always be my favorite—Dad and Grampa had our entire garage covered with the STP 43. Richard and Kyle and the whole Petty family are such kind people and great role models.

—Steven

My total favorite driver is Jeff Gordon because he has a great personality. No matter what, he always has his spirits up—even if he loses a race. I really want to be like him one day—just not the racing part!

—Sharnelle

Dale Earnhardt Jr. has a lot of passion and determination and that's why he is my favorite driver. I admire the way Dale Jr. continued with his dream even after his father died. My favorite NASCAR memory is when he won his first race after his father's death. I was so relieved to see Dale Jr. back on the track and winning that it gave me hope that I could overcome whatever I might face in life just like he did.

—LuLu

ATLANTA
MOTOR SPEEDWAY

1500 HIGHWAY 19 & 41 SOUTH
HAMPTON, GEORGIA

www.atlantamotorspeedway.com

> "What does it take to be a great driver? Ability, determination, guts and a HEAVY FOOT."
>
> —A.J. FOYT

 hosts two **NASCAR NEXTEL** Cup races a year and two words best describe what to expect in Atlanta: Pure Speed.

Atlanta's turns are banked at 24 degrees and, combined with a recent reconfiguration and repaving, **NASCAR'S** elite can rip through the corners and straightaways at blinding speeds.

15

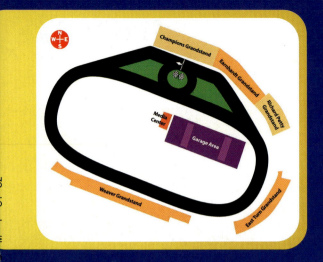

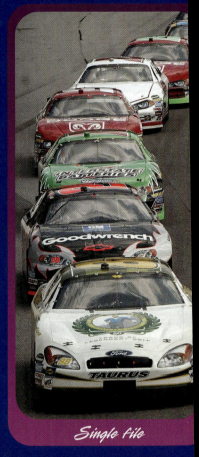

Single file

TrackFacts

Length: 1.54 miles (325 laps = 500.5 miles)

Race Length: 500 miles (1), 500 miles (2)

Frontstretch: 2,332 feet/5°

Backstretch: 1,800 feet/5°

Grandstand Seating Capacity: 124,000

Banking: All turns—24°

First Race: July 31, 1960—Dixie 300

Qualifying & Race Records

Qualifying: Geoffrey Bodine, Ford, 197.478 mph (28.074 sec.); Nov. 15, 1997

Race: Bobby Labonte, Pontiac, 159.904 mph (3:07:48); Nov. 16, 1997

Most Wins: 9—Dale Earnhardt

Oldest Winner: Morgan Shepherd, 51 Years, 4 Months, 27 Days, Mar. 20, 1993

Youngest Winner: Jeff Gordon, 23 Years, 7 Months, 8 Days, Mar. 12, 1995

Most Cautions: 11—three times, most recently, Nov. 14, 1993

TRIVIA

1 Atlanta Motor Speedway is:
- **A** 3.0 Miles
- **B** 1.54 Miles
- **C** 8.04 Miles
- **D** 2.02 Miles

2 Seating capacity at Atlanta Motor Speedway is:
- **A** 1 Million
- **B** 750,000
- **C** 52,000
- **D** 124,000

3 The driver with the most wins at Atlanta Motor Speedway is:
- **A** Richard Petty
- **B** Bobby Allison
- **C** Jeff Gordon
- **D** Dale Earnhardt

4 The driver with the most top 5 finishes at Atlanta Motor Speedway is:
- **A** Richard Petty
- **B** Bobby Allison
- **C** Jeff Gordon
- **D** Dale Earnhardt

5 The oldest winner at 51, at Atlanta Motor Speedway is:
- **A** Cale Yarborough
- **B** Bill Elliott
- **C** Morgan Shepard
- **D** Elliott Sadler

6 The driver with the most laps lead in a 500 mile race at Atlanta Motor Speedway was:
- **A** Cale Yarborough (308 laps)
- **B** Bill Elliott (205 laps)
- **C** Morgan Shepard (285 laps)
- **D** Dale Earnhardt (190 laps)

7 The driver with the most top ten finishes at Atlanta Motor Speedway is:
- **A** Richard Petty (33)
- **B** Dale Earnhardt (26)
- **C** Neil Bonnett (20)
- **D** Jeff Gordon (9)

8 Fewest laps lead by a winner at Atlanta Motor Speedway:
- **A** 8
- **B** 19
- **C** 1
- **D** 4

9 Who did Kevin Harvick beat in 2001 in the closest margin of victory (0.0006) ever at Atlanta Motor Speedway?
- **A** Dale Earnhardt
- **B** Bobby Labonte
- **C** Tony Stewart
- **D** Jeff Gordon

10 What manufacturer has the most victories, with 30, at Atlanta Motor Speedway?
- **A** Ford
- **B** Chevrolet
- **C** Dodge
- **D** Pontiac

M U B P

To bang into an opponent

_____

I L L A S N O

A famous racing family

_____

S A N P G S I

To move by an opponent

_____

C S U F S F

Tires on car during practice for only one or two laps

_____

T A R E T S R

To begin again

_____

RACE #1

Date: _____

Race Name: _____

How's The Weather? _____
_____
_____

Pole Winner: _____

My driver's qualifying time and starting position were: _____

In the Pits: _____
_____
_____

My driver led _____ laps. There were _____ cautions.

My driver finished _____

_____ won the race.

My driver's point standings after the race: _____
_____

Who's the points leader now? _____

It was awesome when: _____
_____
_____

It was SO NOT COOL when: _____
_____
_____

I'll remember this race, because: _____
_____
_____

I went to the race with/watched it on TV with: _____
_____

We stayed at: _____

We had dinner at: _____

We tailgated and had: _____

New friends I met at the race are: _____
_____

What this race meant to me:

_____
_____
_____
_____
_____

RACE #2

Date: _____

Race Name: _____

How's The Weather? _____
_____
_____

Pole Winner: _____

My driver's qualifying time and starting position were: _____

In the Pits: _____
_____
_____

My driver led _____ laps. There were _____ cautions.

My driver finished _____
_____ won the race.

My driver's point standings after the race: _____
_____

Who's the points leader now? _____

It was awesome when: _____
_____
_____

It was SO NOT COOL when: _____
_____
_____

I'll remember this race, because: _____
_____
_____

I went to the race with/watched it on TV with: _____
_____

We stayed at: _____

We had dinner at: _____

We tailgated and had: _____

New friends I met at the race are: _____
_____

What this race meant to me:
_____
_____
_____
_____
_____
_____

NASCAR's an inspiration . . .

I am on my cross country team at school. Sometimes when I am in the middle of a race and starting to feel tired, I think about what NASCAR drivers go through every week racing hundreds of miles in a car without air conditioning, and it gives me the motivation to not give up and to push just a little harder.

Blaine

During one of the races, I saw the "Let's Roll" logo painted on the hood of Bobby Labonte's car. I asked my dad why it was there and he told me that it was a tribute to some of the people who died on September 11. The next day, I asked my teacher about it and he had our whole class research the importance of those words. Because of NASCAR and Bobby Labonte, we learned about Todd Beamer and the other brave people who died on that airplane in Pennsylvania. It was so inspiring that it made me cry.

Robert

NASCAR inspires me because...

_____

_____

_____

_____

_____

_____

_____

_____

RED, WHITE AND BLUE . . . FOREVER

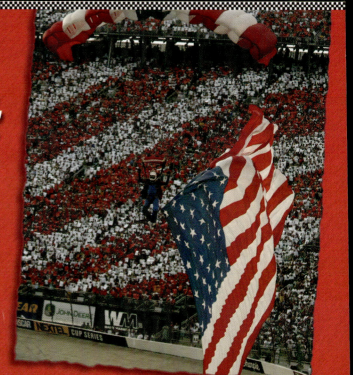

PUSHING THROUGH!

BRISTOL
MOTOR SPEEDWAY

151 SPEEDWAY BLVD.
BRISTOL, TENNESSEE

www.bristolmotorspeedway.com

> "Bristol is my favorite short track."
>
> —RUSTY WALLACE

For **NASCAR** fans, going to  is the must-do road trip of a lifetime!

Bristol is the smallest track on the circuit and many have compared it to watching a **NASCAR** race in the bottom of mixing bowl. Its steep grandstands and intensely banked turns give fans the ultimate **NASCAR** viewing experience!

Yea! The sound is deafening, and we're not even talking about the cars. The action's intense. Think about trying to race forty-three of the most powerful race cars in the world around your school gym and you start to get the idea of what it's like.

Awesome crowds, a tight track and **NASCAR**, what more could you want?

"It's Bristol . . . Baby!"

TrackFacts

Length:	.533 Mile
	(500 laps = 266.5 miles)
Race Length:	500 Laps (1), 500 Laps (2)
Backstretch:	650 feet/16°
Frontstretch:	650 feet/16°
Grandstand Seating Capacity:	160,000
Banking:	All turns—36°
First Race:	July 30, 1961—Volunteer 500

Qualifying & Race Records

Qualifying:	Ryan Newman, Dodge, 128.709 mph (14.908 sec.); March 21, 2003
Race:	Charlie Glotzbach; Chevrolet, 101.075 mph (2:38:12); July 11, 1971
Most Wins:	12—Darrell Waltrip
Oldest Winner:	Dale Earnhardt, 48 Years, 3 Months, 30 Days, Aug. 28, 1999
Youngest Winner:	Kurt Busch, 23 Years, 7 Months, 20 Days, Mar. 24, 2002
Most Cautions:	20—three times, most recently, Aug. 23, 2003

TRIVIA

1 Bristol Motor Speedway is:

    A 1 Mile   **B** 2.41 Miles   **C** .533 Miles   **D** .874 Miles

2 The *NASCAR NEXTEL* Cup races held at Bristol Motor Speedway are:

    A 400 laps   **B** 500 laps   **C** 600 laps   **D** 250 laps

3 The first race at Bristol Motor Speedway was in:

    A 1948   **B** 1971   **C** 1978   **D** 1961

4 The turns at Bristol Motor Speedway are banked at what degree?

    A 36 degrees   **C** 4 degrees

    B 18 degrees   **D** 60 degrees

5 In 2003, who established the qualifying record at Bristol Motor Speedway?

    A Dale Earnhardt Jr.   **C** Kevin Harvick

    B Matt Kenseth   **D** Ryan Newman

6 The Bristol Motor Speedway has a seating capacity of how many?

    A 58,000   **B** 160,000   **C** 90,000   **D** 102,000

7 The driver with the most wins at Bristol Motor Speedway is:

    A Richard Petty   **C** Darrell Waltrip

    B Dale Earnhardt   **D** Jeff Gordon

8 How many did he win?

    A 8   **B** 4   **C** 21   **D** 12

9 The most laps lead in a 500 miles race by a race winner was:

    A 430 by Richard Petty   **C** 500 by Cale Yarborough

    B 275 by Kurt Busch   **D** 182 by Tony Stewart

10 In 2003, who won both races held at Bristol Motor Speedway?

    A Tony Stewart   **C** Jeff Gordon

    B Rusty Wallace   **D** Kurt Busch

WORD SCRAMBLE

T N O R E R F N T C T H

Main straight section of track

_____

N M I

Victory

_____

N O D T A Y A

Where it all began

_____

C N A T C B R E K T H

Opposite the main straight section

_____

G A L N T D N O R I

One of the oldest tracks

_____

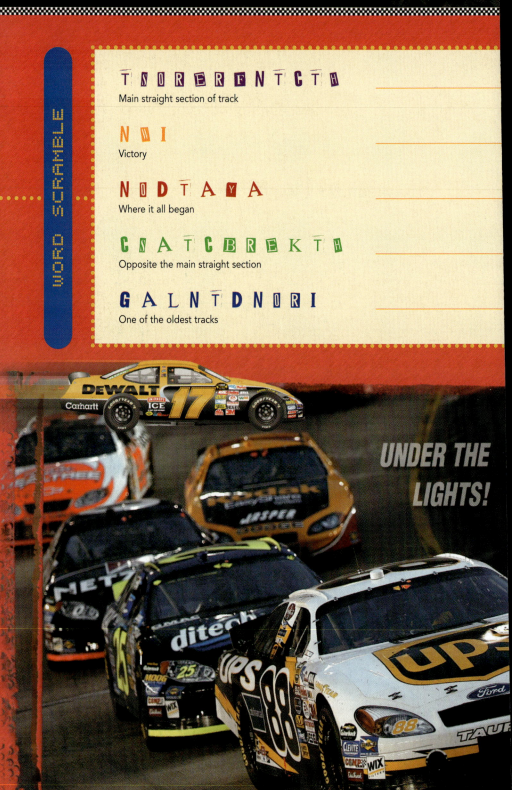

UNDER THE
LIGHTS!

RACE #1

Date: _____

Race Name: _____

How's The Weather? _____

_____

_____

Pole Winner: _____

My driver's qualifying time and starting position were: _____

In the Pits: _____

_____

_____

My driver led _____ laps. There were _____ cautions.

My driver finished _____

_____ won the race.

My driver's point standings after the race: _____

_____

Who's the points leader now? _____

It was awesome when: _____

_____

_____

It was SO NOT COOL when: _____

_____

_____

I'll remember this race, because: _____

_____

_____

I went to the race with/watched it on TV with: _____

_____

We stayed at: _____

We had dinner at: _____

We tailgated and had: _____

New friends I met at the race are: _____

_____

What this race meant to me:

_____

_____

_____

_____

_____

_____

RACE #2

Date: _____

Race Name: _____

How's The Weather? _____
_____
_____

Pole Winner: _____

My driver's qualifying time and starting position were: _____

In the Pits: _____
_____
_____

My driver led _____ laps. There were _____ cautions.

My driver finished _____
_____ won the race.

My driver's point standings after the race: _____
_____

Who's the points leader now? _____

It was awesome when: _____
_____
_____

It was SO NOT COOL when: _____
_____
_____

I'll remember this race, because: _____
_____
_____

I went to the race with/watched it on TV with: _____
_____

We stayed at: _____

We had dinner at: _____

We tailgated and had: _____

New friends I met at the race are: _____
_____

What this race meant to me:
_____
_____
_____
_____
_____
_____

CALIFORNIA
SPEEDWAY

9300 CHERRY AVE. • FONTANA, CALIFORNIA

www.californiaspeedway.com

> "Make the fans comfortable,
> give them a good show, and give
> them their money's worth."
>
> —CLAY EARLES, FOUNDER MARTINSVILLE SPEEDWAY

California residents are perhaps more in love with cars then any other state in the USA so it's only fitting that back in 1997 they hopped on board the *NASCAR* craze and brought the world's greatest sport to the land of sun and fun.

Bring the sun screen and shades, dude, because watching *NASCAR* at *CALIFORNIA SPEEDWAY* means catching a wave of power and excitement in a way that only the Golden State could deliver. A smooth, fast, almost perfect race track becomes a stage that is set in one of the nicest and most comfortable tracks in the series. This is a serious track for some serious racing.

Time to do a little star gazing, kick back and kick it in gear, it's *NASCAR* racing, California style!

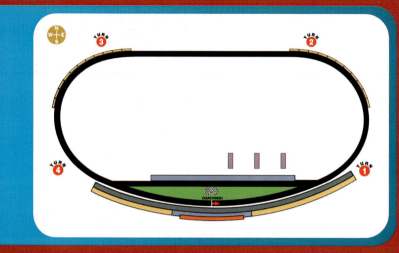

TRACKFACTS

LENGTH:	2 Miles (250 laps = 500 miles)
RACE LENGTH:	500 Miles (1), 500 Miles (2)
BACKSTRETCH:	2,500 feet/3°
FRONTSTRETCH:	3,100 feet/11°
GRANDSTAND SEATING CAPACITY:	92,000
BANKING:	All turns—14°
FIRST RACE:	June 22, 1997—California 500

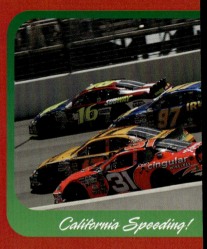

California Speeding!

QUALIFYING & RACE RECORDS

QUALIFYING:	Ryan Newman, Ford, 187.432 mph (38.414 sec.); April 26, 2002
RACE:	Jeff Gordon, Chevrolet, 155.012 mph (3:13:32); June 22, 1997
MOST WINS:	2—Jeff Gordon
OLDEST WINNER:	Rusty Wallace, 44 Years, 8 Months, 15 Days, April 29, 2001
YOUNGEST WINNER:	Kurt Busch, 24 Years, 8 Months, 23 Days, April 27, 2003
MOST CAUTIONS:	8—April 27, 2003

TRIVIA

1 When was the first race held at California Speedway?

Ⓐ 1999   Ⓑ 1987   Ⓒ 1997   Ⓓ 2002

2 Who holds the 2002 California Speedway qualifying record with a speed of 187.432 mph?

Ⓐ Ryan Newman   Ⓒ Rusty Wallace

Ⓑ Casey Mears   Ⓓ Jimmy Johnson

3 California Speedway is located in what town?

Ⓐ Los Angeles   Ⓑ Santa Barbara   Ⓒ Fontana   Ⓓ Irvine

4 The winner of the 2002 race at California Speedway was?

Ⓐ Jimmie Johnson   Ⓒ Brendan Gaughan

Ⓑ Robby Gordon   Ⓓ Bill Elliott

5 The turns at California Speedway are banked at what?

Ⓐ 36 degrees   Ⓑ 14 degrees   Ⓒ 21 degrees   Ⓓ 19 degrees

6 "Loose" causes a car to:

Ⓐ Slow down   Ⓑ Speed up   Ⓒ Fishtail   Ⓓ Fall back a lap

7 A car is "tight" if:

Ⓐ It is hard to steer   Ⓒ Cars are bunched together

Ⓑ The shocks are hard   Ⓓ The engine will not shift gears

8 Dirty air means:

Ⓐ Air pollution   Ⓒ Air turbulence from passing car

Ⓑ Clogged radio airwaves   Ⓓ Heavy smoke

9 A fabricator:

Ⓐ Tells lies   Ⓒ Builds the engine

Ⓑ Matches sheet metal to the frame   Ⓓ Fuels the car at pit stops

10 A gasket is:

Ⓐ A seal between two engine parts   Ⓒ A particular type of wrench

Ⓑ A medical term   Ⓓ A unit of measurement

FRIENDS: TONY STEWART & DALE EARNHARDT, JR.

WORD SCRAMBLE

O A T C I U N
Yellow flag

_____

D D E O G
Ram tough

_____

A K M J A N C
Crewmember who lifts car

_____

A L E D P L A
Not behind (2 words)

_____

N H J O N O N
Jimmie's last name

_____

RYAN NEWMAN

RACE #1

Date: _____

Race Name: _____

How's The Weather? _____

_____

_____

Pole Winner: _____

My driver's qualifying time and starting position were: _____

In the Pits: _____

_____

_____

My driver led _____ laps. There were _____ cautions.

My driver finished _____

_____ won the race.

My driver's point standings after the race: _____

_____

Who's the points leader now? _____

It was awesome when: _____

_____

_____

It was SO NOT COOL when: _____

_____

_____

I'll remember this race, because: _____

_____

_____

I went to the race with/watched it on TV with: _____

_____

We stayed at: _____

We had dinner at: _____

We tailgated and had: _____

New friends I met at the race are: _____

_____

What this race meant to me:

_____

_____

_____

_____

_____

RACE #2

Date: _____
Race Name: _____
How's The Weather? _____
_____
_____

Pole Winner: _____
My driver's qualifying time and starting position were: _____

In the Pits: _____
_____
_____

My driver led _____ laps. There were _____ cautions.

My driver finished _____

_____ won the race.

My driver's point standings after the race: _____
_____

Who's the points leader now? _____

It was awesome when: _____
_____
_____

It was SO NOT COOL when: _____
_____
_____

I'll remember this race, because: _____
_____
_____

I went to the race with/watched it on TV with: _____
_____

We stayed at: _____
We had dinner at: _____
We tailgated and had: _____
New friends I met at the race are: _____
_____

What this race meant to me:
_____
_____
_____
_____
_____
_____
_____

CHICAGOLAND
SPEEDWAY

500 SPEEDWAY BLVD.
JOLIET, ILLINOIS

www.chicagolandspeedway.com

> "There's no bigger surprise than to be tooling along at 200 mph and suddenly getting hit from the rear."
>
> —DARRELL WALTRIP

Chicago is a land of big shoulders and big dreams. With the debut of the Tropicana 400 in 2001, the Windy City became the newest city to host the world of **NASCAR** racing. Kevin Harvick won that inaugural race when he out-dueled Robert Pressley by only 0.649 second.

Sure, Kevin probably gripped the steering wheel a little tighter than normal and with good reason!  *CHICAGOLAND SPEEDWAY*, like the city she calls home, is one great, big place to go bumper to bumper at nearly 200 miles per hour.

Strap in tight because we're about to go racing in Chicagoland!

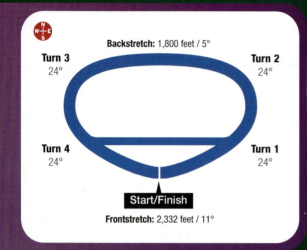

Backstretch: 1,800 feet / 5°

Turn 3
24°

Turn 2
24°

Turn 4
24°

Turn 1
24°

Start/Finish

Frontstretch: 2,332 feet / 11°

Perseverance

TrackFacts

Length:	1.5 Miles (267 laps = 400 miles)
Race Length:	400 Miles
Frontstretch:	2,332 feet / 11°
Backstretch:	1,800 feet / 5°
Grandstand Seating Capacity:	75,000
Banking:	All turns—24°
First Race:	July 15, 2001—Tropicana 400

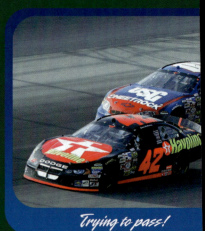

Trying to pass!

Qualifying & Race Records

Qualifying:	Tony Stewart, Chevrolet, 184.786 mph (29.223 sec.); July 11, 2003
Race:	Kevin Harvick, Chevrolet, 136.832 mph (2:55:37); July 14, 2002
Most Wins:	2—Kevin Harvick
Oldest Winner:	Kevin Harvick, 26 Years, 7 Months, 6 Days, July 14, 2002
Youngest Winner:	Ryan Newman, 25 Years, 7 Months, 5 Days, July 13, 2003
Most Cautions:	10—July 15, 2001

TRIVIA

1 Chicagoland Speedway is located in what city?

   Ⓐ Elmhurst   Ⓑ Chicago   Ⓒ Naperville   Ⓓ Joliet

2 What year was the first race held at Chicagoland Speedway?

   Ⓐ 1999   Ⓑ 2003   Ⓒ 2004   Ⓓ 2001

3 The turns at Chicagoland Speedway are banked at how many degrees?

   Ⓐ 60 degrees   Ⓑ 4 degrees   Ⓒ 18 degrees   Ⓓ 24 degrees

4 The seating capacity of Chicagoland Speedway is:

   Ⓐ 24,000   Ⓑ 60,000   Ⓒ 32,000   Ⓓ 75,000

5 Who holds the July 2003 qualifying record of 184.786 mph at Chicagoland Speedway?

   Ⓐ Jeff Gordon   Ⓒ Tony Stewart

   Ⓑ Dale Earnhardt Jr.   Ⓓ Kevin Harvick

6 Who holds the July 2002 race record of 136.832 mph at Chicagoland Speedway?

   Ⓐ Jeff Gordon   Ⓒ Tony Stewart

   Ⓑ Dale Earnhardt Jr.   Ⓓ Kevin Harvick

7 Who won two of the first three races at Chicagoland Speedway?

   Ⓐ Kevin Harvick   Ⓒ Kyle Petty

   Ⓑ Ryan Newman   Ⓓ Sterling Marlin

8 Who went 463 starts before his first victory at the 2001 Daytona 500:

   Ⓐ Sterling Marlin   Ⓒ Kenny Wallace

   Ⓑ Michael Waltrip   Ⓓ Jimmy Spencer

9 Who won the 2004 race at Chicagoland Speedway?

   Ⓐ Scott Wimmer   Ⓒ Tony Stewart

   Ⓑ Brian Vickers   Ⓓ Elliott Sadler

10 "Flat-out" means:

   Ⓐ Being totally exhausted   Ⓒ Missing a crew member

   Ⓑ Racing as fast as possible   Ⓓ Out of money/no sponsor

MAYFIELD ON A CHARGE

WORD SCRAMBLE

R U C R B A T R O A
_____

Where air and fuel mix

N E S H T K E
_____

2003 NASCAR Cup Champion

L M E T R E T E Y
_____

Transmitting sensors

A R I M D A
_____

Keeps front end stable (2 words)

E T S P U
_____

How a car is prepared (2 words)

RACE #1

Date: _____

Race Name: _____

How's The Weather? _____

_____

_____

Pole Winner: _____

My driver's qualifying time and starting position were: _____

_____

In the Pits: _____

_____

_____

My driver led _____ laps. There were _____ cautions.

My driver finished _____

_____ won the race.

My driver's point standings after the race: _____

_____

Who's the points leader now? _____

It was awesome when: _____

_____

_____

It was SO NOT COOL when: _____

_____

_____

I'll remember this race, because: _____

_____

_____

I went to the race with/watched it on TV with: _____

_____

We stayed at: _____

We had dinner at: _____

We tailgated and had: _____

New friends I met at the race are: _____

_____

What this race meant to me:

_____

_____

_____

_____

_____

_____

_____

F	U	E	L	B	M	D	R	I	V	E	R	S
M	E	C	H	A	N	I	C	R	K	L	U	U
U	A	W	V	N	C	R	A	S	H	H	S	P
B	D	R	A	G	D	E	M	R	F	I	T	E
P	O	G	L	A	P	T	B	C	P	F	Y	R
R	S	T	P	I	T	M	E	N	P	M	A	S
W	I	N	B	T	N	W	R	A	O	T	G	P
I	B	A	S	C	U	F	F	S	K	I	L	E
V	I	C	T	O	R	Y	T	C	A	R	B	E
A	L	F	O	R	D	Q	S	A	W	E	Z	D
L	B	C	V	I	C	K	E	R	S	S	A	W
V	J	G	R	E	E	N	F	L	A	G	Y	A
E	A	R	N	H	A	R	D	T	B	M	O	Y

CAR
DRAG
DRIVERS
EARNHARDT
CAMBER
CRASH
FORD
GREENFLAG
LAP
MARLIN
MECHANIC
NASCAR
PIT
RPM
RUSTY
SCUFFS
SUPERSPEEDWAY
TIRES
VALVE
VICKERS
VICTORY
WIN

©1989 Mike Smith. Reprinted by permission.

DARLINGTON
RACEWAY

1301 HARRY BYRD HIGHWAY
DARLINGTON, SOUTH CAROLINA

www.darlingtonraceway.com

> "At Darlington, you don't race against the other drivers. You run against the track."
>
> —RICHARD PETTY

DARLINGTON RACEWAY is like the big kid on the bus who seems to have been in seventh grade forever. You don't want to rub him the wrong way or you're in for a long day.

Darlington has not been around forever, it only feels that way. Built in 1950, the track—known as the track that's "too tough to tame"—has earned its reputation by putting nearly every young upstart *(and a few old ones too)* in their place with a simple kiss of reality against her paint scrapped walls.

Watch your step here; this southern lady doesn't take kindly to anything less than the best.

Turn 3

Turn 4

Turn 2

Turn 1

Colvin Grandstand

Brasington Grandstand

NASCAR Busch Series Garage

Pearson Tower

Victory Lane

NASCAR NEXTEL Cup Series Garage

Wallace Grandstand

Tyler Tower

Media Center

TrackFacts

LENGTH: 1.366 Miles (367 laps = 501.3 miles, 293 laps = 400.2 miles)

RACE LENGTH: 400 Miles (1), 500 Miles (2)

FRONTSTRETCH: 1,229 feet/2°

BACKSTRETCH: 1,229 feet/2°

GRANDSTAND SEATING CAPACITY: 60,000

BANKING: Turns 1 and 2—25° • Turns 3 and 4—23°

FIRST RACE: Sept. 4, 1950—Southern 500

Crowd in the pits

Qualifying & Race Records

QUALIFYING: Ward Burton, Pontiac, 173.797 mph (28.295 sec.); March 22, 1996

RACE: 400 Miles—David Pearson, Ford, 132.703 mph (3:34:55); May 11, 1968

500 Miles—Dale Earnhardt, Chevrolet, 139.958 mph (3:00:54); Mar. 28, 199?

MOST WINS: 10—David Pearson

OLDEST WINNER: Harry Gant, 51 Years, 7 Months, 22 Days, Sept. 1, 1991

YOUNGEST WINNER: Terry Labonte, 23 Years, 9 Months, 16 Days, Sept. 1, 1980

MOST CAUTIONS: 15—March 26, 1995

TRIVIA

1 When was the first race at Darlington Raceway?

Ⓐ 1910　　Ⓑ 1980　　Ⓒ 1950　　Ⓓ 1965

2 How long is Darlington Raceway?

Ⓐ 8 miles　　Ⓑ 1.366 miles　　Ⓒ 2.44 miles　　Ⓓ 1.8 miles

3 What is the degree of banking in turns 1 and 2?

Ⓐ 17 degrees　　Ⓒ 40 degrees

Ⓑ 4 degrees　　Ⓓ 25 degrees

4 What is the degree of banking in turns 3 and 4?

Ⓐ Same as turns 1 and 2　　Ⓒ 17 degrees

Ⓑ 23 degrees　　Ⓓ 20 degrees

5 Who has the most wins at Darlington Raceway?

Ⓐ Richard Petty　　Ⓒ David Person

Ⓑ Jeff Gordon　　Ⓓ Junior Johnson

6 As of 2003, what were the fewest laps led by a race winner and who was he?

Ⓐ Terry Labonte (4 laps)　　Ⓒ Jeff Burton (14 laps)

Ⓑ Sterlin Marlin (8 laps)　　Ⓓ Ricky Craven (1 lap)

7 Who won the 2004 Carolina Dodge Dealers 400 at Darlington Raceway?

Ⓐ Kasey Kahne　　Ⓒ Jimmy Johnson

Ⓑ Terry Labonte　　Ⓓ Dale Earnhardt Jr.

8 NEXTEL became the series sponsor in what year?

Ⓐ 1984　　Ⓑ 2004　　Ⓒ 2000　　Ⓓ 2002

9 What is the banking on the backstretch at Darlington Raceway?

Ⓐ 2 degrees　　Ⓑ 8 degrees　　Ⓒ 6 degrees　　Ⓓ 5 degrees

10 What car owner has the most wins at Darlington Raceway?

Ⓐ Rick Hendrick　　Ⓒ Jack Roush

Ⓑ Junior Johnson　　Ⓓ Roger Penske

WAITING FOR GREEN!

ELLIOTT SADLER

N T A T L A A
A track

_____

A N C A N R
Governing Body

_____

I T P
Driver's stop

_____

D H A R E A T R N
Legend

_____

T O P R T S E
Driver's eyes

_____

RACE #1

Date: _____

Race Name: _____

How's The Weather? _____

_____

_____

Pole Winner: _____

My driver's qualifying time and starting position were: _____

_____

In the Pits: _____

_____

_____

My driver led _____ laps. There were _____ cautions.

My driver finished _____

_____ won the race.

My driver's point standings after the race: _____

_____

Who's the points leader now? _____

It was awesome when: _____

_____

_____

It was SO NOT COOL when: _____

_____

_____

I'll remember this race, because: _____

_____

_____

I went to the race with/watched it on TV with: _____

_____

We stayed at: _____

We had dinner at: _____

We tailgated and had: _____

New friends I met at the race are: _____

_____

What this race meant to me:

_____

_____

_____

_____

_____

If I could hang out with Tony Stewart for a day, I would ask him to show me how his pit crew changes a wheel on his car so fast when it is flat or loses its tread. Then I would have him let me sit beside him in his car while he drives it around the track at 110 mph. That's my dream, even though my mom would never let me be a NASCAR driver—I'm lucky that she even let me go in a simulator!

Geoffrey

If I could hang out with Dale Earnhardt, Jr. for a day I would invite him to my house, so he could see my NASCAR collection—my pictures and ticket stubs and souvenirs. Then, I would go to his house and see his NASCAR collection, including his car! He would give me driving lessons and also let me drive his car. We would go to a NASCAR race, and I would get to hang out in his pit and help his crew during pit stops. Of course, Mr. Earnhardt would win the race, and I would get to celebrate with him. It would be the best day of my life!

Jack

If I could work in the pit for a day, I'd want to . . .

_____

_____

_____

_____

_____

DAYTONA
INTERNATIONAL SPEEDWAY

1801 W. INTERNATIONAL SPEEDWAY BLVD. DAYTONA BEACH, FLORIDA

www.daytonainternationalspeedway.com

> "Daytona has brought racing up to the standard it is today. The whole sport has grown around the Daytona Speedway."
>
> —LEE PETTY

Fame, history, high banking, long straightaways, roaring crowds—*man,* it can only be *DAYTONA INTERNATIONAL SPEEDWAY*.

Go ahead, breathe in the salty air and let your imagination drift back to where it all began. Picture guys with their souped-up family wagons, tearing down the beaches like speed demons. Yea that's right, *on Daytona Beach,* trying to beat out equally crazy competitors and most of all, the high tide.

Now, almost half a century later, Daytona is still the place to be for the best in *NASCAR* racing. Home of the Daytona 500, *Speedweeks*— the ultimate family road trip, and the Pepsi 400, this place is built for speed and . . . it delivers.

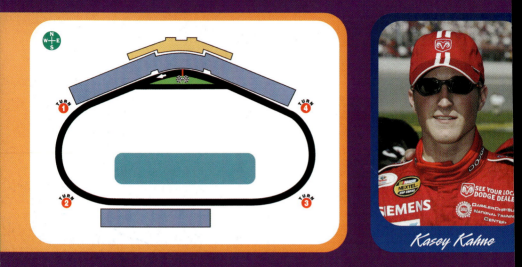

Kasey Kahne

TrackFacts

LENGTH:	2.5 Miles (200 laps = 500 miles, 160 laps = 400 miles)
RACE LENGTH:	500 Miles (1), 400 Miles (2)
FRONTSTRETCH:	3,800 feet/18°
BACKSTRETCH:	3,400 feet/3°
GRANDSTAND SEATING CAPACITY:	168,000
BANKING:	All turns 31°
FIRST RACE:	Feb. 22, 1959—Daytona 500

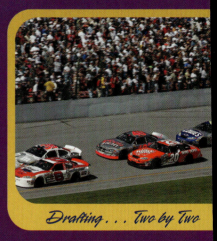

Drafting . . . Two by Two

QUALIFYING & RACE RECORDS

QUALIFYING:	Bill Elliott, Ford, 210.364 mph (42.783 sec.); Feb. 9, 1987
RACE:	400 Miles—Bobby Allison, Mercury, 173.473 mph (2:18:21); July 4, 1980
	500 Miles—Buddy Baker, Oldsmobile, 177.602 mph (2:48:55); Feb. 17, 1980
MOST WINS:	10—Richard Petty
OLDEST WINNER:	Bobby Allison, 50 Years, 2 Months, 11 Days, Feb. 14, 1988
YOUNGEST WINNER:	Jeff Gordon, 23 Years, 10 Months, 27 Days, July 1, 1995
MOST CAUTIONS:	12—July 1, 1989

TRIVIA

1 Stock car races used to be held *on* Daytona Beach.

   A True   **B** False

2 The two weeks of racing activity that culminates with the Daytona 500 is called:

   A Speedweeks   **C** The Need for Speed

   B The Countdown   **D** Daytona Days

3 The banking in turns 1 and 2 at Daytona International Speedway are:

   A 19 degrees   **C** 31 degrees

   B 24 degrees   **D** 10 degrees

4 The banking in turns 3 and 4 at Daytona International Speedway are:

   A 24 degrees   **C** 10 degrees

   B 19 degrees   **D** Same as turns 1 and 2

5 Daytona International Speedway is a:

   A Road Course   **B** Tri-oval   **C** Square   **D** Oval

6 Daytona International Speedway is how long?

   A 1.44 miles   **B** 3.02 miles   **C** 2.5 miles   **D** 2.0 miles

7 Daytona International Speedway is 70 miles northeast of what city?

   A Raleigh   **B** Miami   **C** Tampa   **D** Orlando

8 In 1987, the 210.364 mph qualifying record was set by which driver?

   A Bill Elliott   **C** Rusty Wallace

   B Dale Earnhardt   **D** Richard Petty

9 The winner of the 2004 Daytona 500 was:

   A Michael Waltrip   **C** Tony Stewart

   B Brian Vickers   **D** Dale Earnhardt, Jr.

10 The driver with the most wins at Daytona International Speedway is:

   A Richard Petty   **C** Junior Johnson

   B Dale Earnhardt   **D** Bobby Allison

WORD SCRAMBLE

S A C S I H S

Steel frame

_____

I F Q Y N G A I L N

To determine starting position

_____

R C U E H E C F I

Leader of a race team (2 words)

_____

U K S T C R C A

What the car is called (2 words)

_____

A T F R C A R B I U

Team member who molds metal to the frame

_____

LEADING THE WAY

RACE #1

Date: _____

Race Name: _____

How's The Weather? _____
_____
_____

Pole Winner: _____

My driver's qualifying time and starting position were: _____

In the Pits: _____
_____
_____

My driver led _____ laps. There were _____ cautions.

My driver finished _____

_____ won the race.

My driver's point standings after the race: _____

Who's the points leader now? _____

It was awesome when: _____
_____
_____

It was SO NOT COOL when: _____
_____
_____

I'll remember this race, because: _____
_____
_____

I went to the race with/watched it on TV with: _____
_____

We stayed at: _____

We had dinner at: _____

We tailgated and had: _____

New friends I met at the race are: _____
_____

What this race meant to me:

_____
_____
_____
_____
_____
_____

RACE #2

Date: _____

Race Name: _____

How's The Weather? _____
_____
_____

Pole Winner: _____

My driver's qualifying time and starting position were: _____

In the Pits: _____
_____
_____

My driver led _____ laps. There were _____ cautions.

My driver finished _____
_____ won the race.

My driver's point standings after the race: _____
_____

Who's the points leader now? _____

It was awesome when: _____
_____
_____

It was SO NOT COOL when: _____
_____
_____

I'll remember this race, because: _____
_____
_____

I went to the race with/watched it on TV with:
_____

We stayed at: _____

We had dinner at: _____

We tailgated and had: _____

New friends I met at the race are: _____
_____

What this race meant to me:
_____
_____
_____
_____
_____
_____

Family Memories . . .

Sometimes when my dad and I are on the highway, we pretend that my dad is a NASCAR driver and I am his spotter. I tell him what is going on around him, like if it is safe to pass the car ahead of us or if we have to stay where we are. It's a lot of fun and helps us to pass the time.   Buzz

Our family has a camper and we go to two NASCAR races every year. We park our camper in the same place each time, and over the years my family has become friends with the other families that park near us. Mom and Dad love to grill all kinds of great food and all of the families like to share the food that they have made. It's like a huge party! We don't get a lot of sleep during these race trips—but there is plenty of time for that during the rest of the year. I look forward to these trips with my family more than anything.   CJ

Every other Sunday is a special day for me with my dad. He and my mom do not live together any more and I can only visit him every other weekend. I miss my dad so much when I don't get to see him, so that makes our time together even more important to me. I love spending our Sundays watching NASCAR and cheering for our favorite driver, Jeff Gordon. Dad and I call it our "Special Time." He even lets me eat fried chicken on the couch!   Emma

My favorite person to watch NASCAR with is

_____ because _____

_____

_____

_____

_____

_____

_____

LET'S GO CAMPING!

No. 24 PIT CREW

DOVER
INTERNATIONAL SPEEDWAY

1131 N. DUPONT HWY.
DOVER, DELAWARE

www.doverspeedway.com

> "If the lion didn't bite
> the tamer every once in a while,
> it wouldn't be exciting."
>
> —DARRELL WALTRIP

DOVER INTERNATIONAL SPEEDWAY is known as the "Monster Mile" and with good reason: winning here takes some good old fashion guts and determination.

Combine a one-mile, oval track with 24 degrees of banking and a concrete surface and you have a mixture that will try the concentration of even the most hardened competitors.

If you think it's a scary idea to have a monster chasing after you, try staring it right in the face for 400 miles. You know it's out there, and the "monster" is waiting.

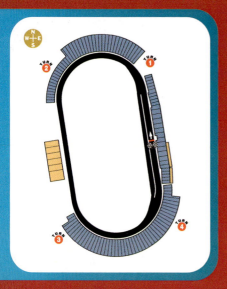

Inside Track

TrackFacts

LENGTH:	1 Mile (400 laps = 400 miles)
RACE LENGTH:	400 Miles (1), 400 Miles (2)
FRONTSTRETCH:	1,076 feet/9°
BACKSTRETCH:	1,076 feet/9°
GRANDSTAND SEATING CAPACITY:	140,000
BANKING:	All turns—24°
FIRST RACE:	July 6, 1969—Mason-Dixon 300

Three Wide Battle

Qualifying & Race Records

QUALIFYING:	Rusty Wallace, Ford, 159.964 mph (22.505 sec.); Sept. 24, 1999
RACE:	Mark Martin, Ford, 132.719 mph (3:00:50); Sept. 21, 1997
MOST WINS:	7—Bobby Allison and Richard Petty
OLDEST WINNER:	Harry Gant, 52 Years, 4 Months, 21 Days, May 31, 1992
YOUNGEST WINNER:	Jeff Gordon, 24 Years, 1 Month, 13 Days, Sept. 17, 1995
MOST CAUTIONS:	16—Sept. 19, 1993

1. The winner of the June 2004 MBNA 400 at Dover International Speedway was:
   - **A** Kasey Kahne
   - **B** Matt Kenseth
   - **C** Mark Martin
   - **D** Elliott Sadler

2. The Dover International Speedway is known as:
   - **A** The Concrete Jungle
   - **B** The House of Speed
   - **C** The Monster Mile
   - **D** The Speedway

3. The banking in the turns at Dover International Speedway are:
   - **A** 2 degrees
   - **B** 24 degrees
   - **C** 18 degrees
   - **D** 14 degrees

4. Two drivers have won the most races at Dover International Speedway.
   - **A** Bobby Allison and Richard Petty
   - **B** Cale Yarborough and David Pearson
   - **C** Dale Earnhardt and Jeff Gordon
   - **D** Rusty Wallace and Darrell Waltrip

5. The record for the fewest cautions in a race at Dover International Speedway was set in 1971. How many cautions were there?
   - **A** 5
   - **B** 0
   - **C** 3
   - **D** 7

6. The seating capacity at Dover International Speedway is:
   - **A** 1 million
   - **B** 32,000
   - **C** 75,000
   - **D** 140,000

7. Bobby Labonte is from what state?
   - **A** Rhode Island
   - **B** North Carolina
   - **C** Texas
   - **D** Indiana

8. Matt Kenseth is from:
   - **A** New Jersey
   - **B** Wisconsin
   - **C** North Dakota
   - **D** Minnesota

9. The winner of the September 2004 MBNA 400 at Dover International Speedway was:
   - **A** Greg Biffle
   - **B** Dale Earnhardt Jr.
   - **C** Ryan Newman
   - **D** Jeff Burton

10. The car owner with the most wins at Dover International Speedway is:
    - **A** Junior Johnson
    - **B** Jack Roush
    - **C** Roger Penske
    - **D** Rick Hendrick

GETTING E

WORD SCRAMBLE

Y D E S O C A N I R A M _____
Air flow over car

P E D S E _____
Can't get enough of it

S T E I I C N N O S P _____
Conducted by officials

A R T D G N E I _____
Single file racing

T P I R N C E _____
They service the car (2 words)

RACE #1

Date: _____

Race Name: _____

How's The Weather? _____

_____

_____

Pole Winner: _____

My driver's qualifying time and starting position were: _____

In the Pits: _____

_____

_____

My driver led _____ laps. There were _____ cautions.

My driver finished _____

_____ won the race.

My driver's point standings after the race: _____

_____

Who's the points leader now? _____

It was awesome when: _____

_____

_____

It was SO NOT COOL when: _____

_____

_____

I'll remember this race, because: _____

_____

_____

I went to the race with/watched it on TV with: _____

_____

We stayed at: _____

We had dinner at: _____

We tailgated and had: _____

New friends I met at the race are: _____

_____

What this race meant to me:

_____

_____

_____

_____

_____

_____

RACE #2

Date: _____

Race Name: _____

How's The Weather? _____

_____

_____

Pole Winner: _____

My driver's qualifying time and starting position were: _____

In the Pits: _____

_____

_____

My driver led _____ laps. There were _____ cautions.

My driver finished _____

_____ won the race.

My driver's point standings after the race: _____

_____

Who's the points leader now? _____

It was awesome when: _____

_____

_____

It was SO NOT COOL when: _____

_____

_____

I'll remember this race, because: _____

_____

_____

I went to the race with/watched it on TV with:

_____

We stayed at: _____

We had dinner at: _____

We tailgated and had: _____

New friends I met at the race are: _____

_____

What this race meant to me:

_____

_____

_____

_____

_____

_____

HOMESTEAD-MIAMI
SPEEDWAY

ONE SPEEDWAY BLVD.
HOMESTEAD, FLORIDA

www.homesteadmiamispeedway.com

> "You've got to have some brakes,
> but you've got to make some
> of your own brakes, too."
>
> JEREMY MAYFIELD

Could it be that the only thing hotter than the non-stop action of **NASCAR** racing is **NASCAR** racing mixed with the South Beach international flare, kickin' fashion and culture of Miami, Florida!

Wow! Beautiful people, beautiful weather, beautiful beaches and the incredible variety of things to do provide any **NASCAR** fan with what could be the most unique experience anywhere in the **NASCAR** series.

So soak in some sun and put on your dancing shoes! **NASCAR** racing at  is a salsa dance of forty-three muscle cars, ripping around a one and a half mile track and the party doesn't stop until there is only one *champion*.

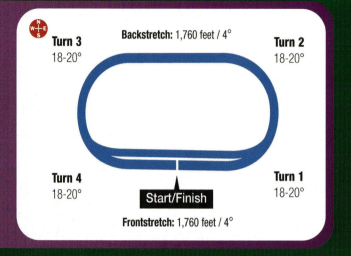

Turn 3
18-20°

Backstretch: 1,760 feet / 4°

Turn 2
18-20°

Turn 4
18-20°

Start/Finish

Turn 1
18-20°

Frontstretch: 1,760 feet / 4°

Scott Wimmer

TRACKFACTS

LENGTH:	1.5 Miles (267 laps = 400.5 miles)
RACE LENGTH:	400 Miles
FRONTSTRETCH:	1,760 feet/4°
BACKSTRETCH:	1,760 feet/4°
GRANDSTAND SEATING CAPACITY:	65,000
BANKING:	All turns—20°
FIRST RACE:	Nov. 14, 1999—Pennzoil 400

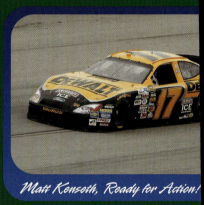

Matt Kenseth, Ready for Action!

QUALIFYING & RACE RECORDS

QUALIFYING:	Jamie McMurray, Dodge, 181.111 mph (29.816 sec.); Nov. 14, 2003
RACE:	Bobby Labonte, Chevrolet, 116.868 mph (3:25:37); Nov. 16, 2003
MOST WINS:	2—Tony Stewart
OLDEST WINNER:	Bill Elliott, 46 Years, 1 Month, 3 Days, Nov. 11, 2001
YOUNGEST WINNER:	Kurt Busch, 24 Years, 3 Months, 13 Days, Nov. 17, 2002
MOST CAUTIONS:	10—Nov. 16, 2003

TRIVIA

1. Miami is famous for what area?

   Ⓐ Mansion Road   Ⓒ Gold Coast

   Ⓑ 17 Mile Drive   Ⓓ South Beach

2. The shape of Homestead-Miami Speedway is:

   Ⓐ Square   Ⓑ Oval   Ⓒ Tri-oval   Ⓓ Circle

3. The first NASCAR race at Homestead-Miami Speedway was held in:

   Ⓐ 1999   Ⓑ 2001   Ⓒ 2003   Ⓓ 1971

4. The winner of that race was:

   Ⓐ Jeff Gordon   Ⓒ Tony Stewart

   Ⓑ Ricky Rudd   Ⓓ Bobby Labonte

5. The seating capacity at Homestead-Miami Speedway is:

   Ⓐ 1 Million   Ⓑ 65,000   Ⓒ 48,000   Ⓓ 18,000

6. The famous island chain about 45 minutes south of Homestead-Miami Speedway are called:

   Ⓐ The Barrier Islands   Ⓒ The Florida Keys

   Ⓑ Hawaii Islands   Ⓓ Tropical Islands

7. The 2002 NASCAR Champion was:

   Ⓐ Dale Earnhardt Jr.   Ⓒ Tony Stewart

   Ⓑ Jeff Gordon   Ⓓ Bill Elliott

8. A NASCAR NEXTEL Cup car has how much horsepower (non-restrictor plate)?

   Ⓐ 1,000 Horsepower   Ⓒ 250 Horsepower

   Ⓑ 790 Horsepower   Ⓓ 325 Horsepower

9. Homestead-Miami Speedway is how long?

   Ⓐ 2.31 Miles   Ⓑ 1.89 Miles   Ⓒ 1.5 Miles   Ⓓ 1.99 Miles

10. The 2003 rookie of the year was:

    Ⓐ Jamie McMurray   Ⓒ Greg Biffle

    Ⓑ Casey Mears   Ⓓ Kasey Kahne

TONY STEWART AND GREG ZIPADELLI

WORD SCRAMBLE

L A N L
Don't want to hit it

_____

S A I E T F G H R
Standard transmissions need one

_____

I C L N B G O K
Positioning to prevent passing

_____

A R G G E A
Work on set up here

_____

R D O G N O
Superstar

_____

RACE #1

Date: _____

Race Name: _____

How's The Weather? _____

_____

_____

Pole Winner: _____

My driver's qualifying time and starting position were: _____

In the Pits: _____

_____

_____

My driver led _____ laps. There were _____ cautions.

My driver finished _____

_____ won the race.

My driver's point standings after the race: _____

_____

Who's the points leader now? _____

It was awesome when: _____

_____

_____

It was SO NOT COOL when: _____

_____

_____

I'll remember this race, because: _____

_____

_____

I went to the race with/watched it on TV with: _____

_____

We stayed at: _____

We had dinner at: _____

We tailgated and had: _____

New friends I met at the race are: _____

_____

What this race meant to me:

_____

_____

_____

_____

_____

_____

```
F R O N T S T R E T C H N
B I M L C Z S T E W A R T
T P N T S T O P V H I M I
A C A S P O T T E R H K G
L A B P P D P O L E F Z H
L R P O N E W C L I D D T
E B A N L H C R E W Z E M
D U X S V I C T O R Y Z H
E R U O V P N W I N H G A
G E A R S J U N I O R I U
A T B C D N E W M A N F L
M O K T E M P L A T E S E
N R I A L T E R N A T O R
```

ALTERNATOR
CARBURETOR
CREW
FRONTRETCH
GEARS
HAULER
INSPECTIONS
JUNIOR
LID
NEWMAN
POLE
SPEED
SPONSOR
SPOTTER
STEWART
STOP
TALLADEGA
TEMPLATES
VICTORY
WIN

©2000 Mark Parisi. Reprinted by permission.

INDIANAPOLIS
MOTOR SPEEDWAY

4790 W. 16TH STREET
INDIANAPOLIS, INDIANAPOLIS

www.indianapolismotorspeedway.com

> "Tough times are the Lord's way
> of teaching me to be strong."
> —GEOFF BODINE

Walk softly and show respect, for you are about to enter auto racing's premier shrine: Indianapolis Motor Speedway. Come worship at this alter of speed and be inspired by this mecca for the racing devoted.

INDIANAPOLIS MOTOR SPEEDWAY, dubbed "The Brickyard" is arguably the most prestigious racetrack in the world. Built in 1909, it is definitely the oldest, continuously operated track in the world and has been host to the legendary Indianapolis 500 forever. But, in 1994 **NASCAR'S** good ol' boys decided to pay a visit and things have never been the same.

Huge crowds, fast turns, pure speed straightaways and the lore of the place all combine to make **NASCAR** at Indianapolis Motor Speedway a happening you've just got to be a part of.

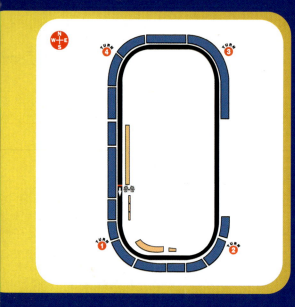

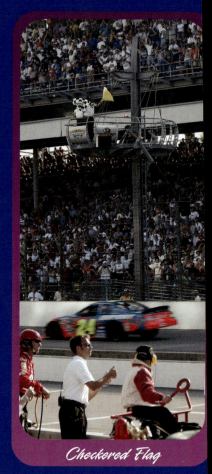

Checkered Flag

TRACKFACTS

LENGTH: 2.5 Miles (160 laps = 400 miles)

RACE LENGTH: 400 Miles

FRONTSTRETCH: 3,300 feet/0°

BACKSTRETCH: 3,300 feet/0°

GRANDSTAND SEATING CAPACITY: 250,000+

BANKING: All Turns—9°

FIRST RACE: Aug. 6, 1994—Brickyard 400

QUALIFYING & RACE RECORDS

QUALIFYING: Kevin Harvick, Chevrolet, 184.343 mph (48.822 sec.); Aug. 2, 2003

RACE: Bobby Labonte, Pontiac, 155.912 mph (2:33:56); Aug. 5, 2000

MOST WINS: 4—Jeff Gordon

OLDEST WINNER: Bill Elliott, 46 Years, 9 Months, 27 Days, Aug. 4, 2002

YOUNGEST WINNER: Jeff Gordon, 23 Years, 2 Days, Aug. 6, 1994

MOST CAUTIONS: 9—Aug. 1, 1998

TRIVIA

1 The first *NASCAR* Cup race held at Indianapolis Motor Speedway was in:

Ⓐ 2001 Ⓑ 1998 Ⓒ 1994 Ⓓ 2002

2 Who won that race?

Ⓐ Jeff Gordon Ⓒ Dale Jarrett
Ⓑ Dale Earnhardt Ⓓ Ken Harvick

3 The driver with the most *NASCAR* wins at Indianapolis Motor Speedway is:

Ⓐ Dale Earnhardt Ⓒ Jeff Gordon
Ⓑ Bobby Labonte Ⓓ Bill Elliott

4 The winner of the 2004 Brickyard 400 at Indianapolis Motor Speedway was:

Ⓐ Dale Earnhardt Jr. Ⓒ Kasey Kahne
Ⓑ Casey Mears Ⓓ Jeff Gordon

5 Indianapolis Motor Speedway is located in what state?

Ⓐ Kansas Ⓒ Illinois
Ⓑ Indiana Ⓓ North Carolina

6 The seating capacity at Indianapolis Motor Speedway is:

Ⓐ 1 Million Ⓑ 250,000 Ⓒ 225,000 Ⓓ 150,000

7 Indianapolis Motor Speedway is also known as:

Ⓐ The Backyard Ⓒ Camden Yard
Ⓑ The Yard Ⓓ The Brickyard

8 The turns at Indianapolis Motor Speedway are banked at:

Ⓐ 18 degrees Ⓒ 9 degrees
Ⓑ 14 degrees Ⓓ 36 degrees

9 Sunoco became the official fuel of *NASCAR* in:

Ⓐ 2004 Ⓑ 1999 Ⓒ 2001 Ⓓ 2003

10 How many laps does it take to drive 400 miles at Indianapolis Motor Speedway?

Ⓐ 400 laps Ⓑ 195 laps Ⓒ 160 laps Ⓓ 300 laps

COMING DOWN THE FRONTSTRETCH!

M P E T E T S L A
Standardized pieces of metal

_____

L G M A A N F
Waves signals to drivers

_____

O L S E O
Rear of car not gripping

_____

A K N H E
Young star

_____

U L E F L C E L
Gas tank (2 words)

_____

RACE #1

Date: _____
Race Name: _____
How's The Weather? _____
_____
_____

Pole Winner: _____
My driver's qualifying time and starting position were: _____
_____

In the Pits: _____
_____
_____

My driver led _____ laps. There were _____ cautions.
My driver finished _____
_____ won the race.
My driver's point standings after the race: _____
_____
Who's the points leader now? _____

It was awesome when: _____
_____
_____

It was SO NOT COOL when: _____
_____
_____

I'll remember this race, because: _____
_____
_____

I went to the race with/watched it on TV with: _____
_____

We stayed at: _____
We had dinner at: _____
We tailgated and had: _____
New friends I met at the race are: _____
_____

What this race meant to me:
_____
_____
_____
_____
_____

NASCAR is the best sport in the world because it involves team work, strategy and luck. Plus, it is the only sport that our whole family likes to watch together.

Samuel

I love NASCAR because I love to see people show their talent, and do their best time after time, even when they lose. Also, I love seeing Jeff Gordon so happy after a race, no matter what—if he lost or won!

Sharnelle

I love NASCAR because it exhilarates me! I feel excited and happy when I watch the drivers race and they are going really fast. Then, it's really cool when they slow down to celebrate their win or to congratulate another racer. It's kind of like my life. I go really fast and then I take the time to be happy about the good things!

LuLu

NASCAR's a lot like life because . . .

_____
_____
_____
_____
_____
_____
_____
_____
_____

INFINEON
RACEWAY

HIGHWAYS 37 & 121
SONOMA, CALIFORNIA

www.infineonraceway.com

> "We're not lucky.
> We win because we work hard."
> —ROGER PENSKE

In the **NASCAR** family of races since 1989,  brings a number of unique things to the table. First, it's in Sonoma, California and if your parents' enthusiasm for the Sonoma region is any indication, this area is *sweet*. The homes in the area may cost a ton, but hey, we're just passing through and there's plenty of reason to soak up the good life while we do. Next, Infineon Raceway is a road course and you know what that means: some of the most extraordinary **NASCAR** racing you have ever seen *(even right hand turns)*!

Have the butler fetch some snacks. It's time to settle into a life of leisure and breathe in the rarified air kicked up by **NASCAR** racing at Infineon Raceway.

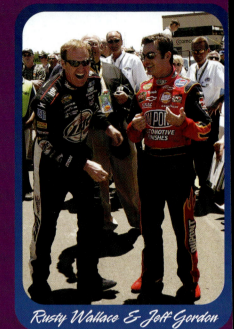

Rusty Wallace & Jeff Gordon

TrackFacts

Length: 1.99 Miles
(110 laps = 218.9 miles/
352.285 kilometers)

Race Length: 350 Kilometers

Frontstretch: N/A

Backstretch: N/A

Grandstand
Seating Capacity: N/A

Banking: N/A

First Race: June 11, 1989—Banquet 300

Getting Air!

Qualifying & Race Records

Qualifying: Boris Said, Pontiac, 93.620 mph (76.522 sec.); June 20, 2003

Race: Ricky Rudd, Ford, 81.007 mph (2:42:08); June 23, 2001

Most Wins: 3—Jeff Gordon

Oldest Winner: Ricky Rudd, 45 Years, 9 Months, 11 Days, June 23, 2002

Youngest Winner: Jeff Gordon, 26 Years, 10 Months, 24 Days, June 28, 1998

Most Cautions: 9—June 10, 1990

TRIVIA

1 Infineon Raceway is located in what state?

Ⓐ North Carolina   Ⓑ Arizona   Ⓒ California   Ⓓ Nevada

2 Infineon Raceway is a:

Ⓐ Circle   Ⓑ Oval   Ⓒ Tri-oval   Ⓓ Road Course

3 Infineon Raceway is:

Ⓐ 2.44 Miles   Ⓑ 1.99 Miles   Ⓒ 1.68 Miles   Ⓓ 1.24 Miles

4 The 2002 rookie of the year was:

Ⓐ Tony Stewart   Ⓒ Casey Mears

Ⓑ Ryan Newman   Ⓓ John Andretti

5 The weight of a **NASCAR NEXTEL** Cup car, without a driver, is:

Ⓐ 2,000 lbs.   Ⓑ 6,000 lbs.   Ⓒ 3,400 lbs.   Ⓓ 8,000 lbs.

6 A black flag means:

Ⓐ You've won!   Ⓑ Caution   Ⓒ Re-start   Ⓓ Return to pits

7 **NASCAR NEXTEL** Cup cars have both a driver and a passenger seat?

Ⓐ True   Ⓑ False

8 Drag is:

Ⓐ Air resistance   Ⓒ Bumped into a wall

Ⓑ Something you do not like   Ⓓ Flat Tire

9 The Catch Can Man:

Ⓐ Handles the media   Ⓒ Collects overflow fuel

Ⓑ Tunes the car's engine   Ⓓ Times the pit stop

10 The winner of the 2004 Dodge/Save Mart 350 at Infineon Raceway was:

Ⓐ Kevin Harvick   Ⓒ Matt Kenseth

Ⓑ Dale Jarrett   Ⓓ Jeff Gordon

WORD SCRAMBLE

S I R T E

_____

Driver wants them to last

E A C P E P A R A N

_____

A chance to meet the fans

E T N X E L P C U

_____

NASCAR'S top circuit (2 words)

G R D A

_____

Aerodynamic force of resistance

I N O J U R

_____

Not senior

INSPECTION

RACE #1

Date: _____

Race Name: _____

How's The Weather? _____

_____

_____

Pole Winner: _____

My driver's qualifying time and starting position were: _____

In the Pits: _____

_____

_____

My driver led _____ laps. There were _____ cautions.

My driver finished _____

_____ won the race.

My driver's point standings after the race: _____

_____

Who's the points leader now? _____

It was awesome when: _____

_____

_____

It was SO NOT COOL when: _____

_____

_____

I'll remember this race, because: _____

_____

_____

I went to the race with/watched it on TV with: _____

_____

We stayed at: _____

We had dinner at: _____

We tailgated and had: _____

New friends I met at the race are: _____

_____

What this race meant to me:

_____

_____

_____

_____

_____

_____

```
C A U T I O N A D R A G W
G A S K E T C F I O E H E
A W R E N C H G B J D D D
U K M B P R U L V N O G G
G T H A U L E T T S W H E
E I X H O R S E P O W E R
Y G A D C F A E R G B L Z
H H I J P I S T O N L M K
O T M S U N S P O I L E R
I G N I T I O N K R P T V
R A X D R A F T I N G T W
B T E M P L A T E Y D Z C
E D R I V E S H A F T G F
```

CARBURATOR
CAUTION
DODGE
DRAFTING
DRAG
DRIVESHAFT
ENGINE
GASKET
GUAGE
HAULER
HELMET
HORSEPOWER
IGNITION
PISTON
ROOKIE
SPOILER
TEMPLATE
TIGHT
WEDGE
WRENCH

I WANT TO SEND SOME FAN MAIL TO JEFF GORDON. WHAT'S HIS ADDRESS?

VICTORY LANE.

SPORTS GORDON WINS DAYTONA 500

UNITED FEATURE SYNDICATE 1999
MIKESMITH
smith@lasvegassun.com

©2000 Mike Smith. Reprinted by permission.

KANSAS
SPEEDWAY

400 SPEEDWAY BLVD.
KANSAS CITY, KANSAS

www.kansasspeedway.com

> "In every aspect of life,
> have a game plan, and then do
> your best to achieve it."
>
> ALAN KULWICKI

In a word,  is *awesome*.

Since hosting its first **NASCAR** event in 2001, Kansas Speedway has given race fans everything they expect from a new, modern raceway. In keeping with the state it calls home, Kansas Speedway is big, bold and beautiful in an understated and completely welcoming sort of way.

Just one trip here and you feel like you're walking around your own backyard. Smooth and comfortable, watching a **NASCAR** race here is like settling into your favorite spot on the couch. Get comfortable, because Kansas Speedway is coming at ya!

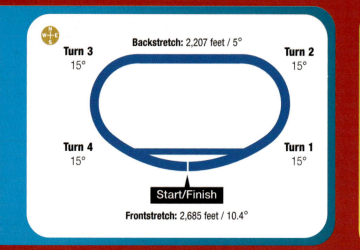

Turn 3
15°

Backstretch: 2,207 feet / 5°

Turn 2
15°

Turn 4
15°

Turn 1
15°

Start/Finish

Frontstretch: 2,685 feet / 10.4°

Inching by!

TRACKFACTS

LENGTH:	1.5 Miles (267 laps = 400 miles)
RACE LENGTH:	400 Miles
FRONTSTRETCH:	2,685 feet/10.4°
BACKSTRETCH:	2,207 feet/5°
GRANDSTAND	
SEATING CAPACITY:	80,187
BANKING:	All Turns—15°
FIRST RACE:	Sept. 30, 2001—Protection One 400

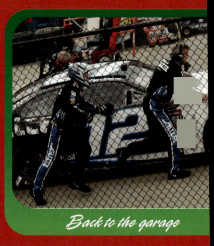

Back to the garage

QUALIFYING & RACE RECORDS

QUALIFYING:	Jimmie Johnson, Chevrolet, 180.373 mph (29.938 sec.); Oct. 3, 2003
RACE:	Ryan Newman, Dodge, 121.630 mph (3:17:34); Oct. 5, 2003
MOST WINS:	2—Jeff Gordon
OLDEST WINNER:	Jeff Gordon, 31 Years, 1 Month, 25 Days, Sept. 29, 2002
YOUNGEST WINNER:	Ryan Newman, 25 Years, 9 Months, 27 Days, Oct. 5, 2003
MOST CAUTIONS:	13—Sept. 30, 2001

TRIVIA

1 Kansas Speedway opened in what year?

Ⓐ 1998   Ⓑ 2003   Ⓒ 2004   Ⓓ 2001

2 Kansas Speedway is how long?

Ⓐ 1.5 Miles   Ⓑ 2.44 Miles   Ⓒ 3.2 Miles   Ⓓ 1.1 Miles

3 Kansas Speedway has what degree of banking in the turns?

Ⓐ 90 degrees   Ⓒ 15 degrees
Ⓑ 20 degrees   Ⓓ 32 degrees

4 The banking on the frontstretch at Kansas Speedway is:

Ⓐ 15 degrees   Ⓒ 10.4 degrees
Ⓑ 12 degrees   Ⓓ 22 degrees

5 Banking on the backstretch at Kansas Speedway is:

Ⓐ 5 degrees   Ⓒ Same as frontstretch
Ⓑ 8 degrees   Ⓓ 19 degrees

6 The length of the frontstretch and the backstretch at Kansas Speedway is the same.

Ⓐ True   Ⓑ False

7 The grandstand seating capacity at Kansas Speedway is:

Ⓐ 62,000   Ⓑ 104,000   Ⓒ 80,187   Ⓓ 48,204

8 In 2004, Joe Nemechek beat this driver by 0.081 seconds:

Ⓐ Elliott Sadler   Ⓒ Jeremy Mayfield
Ⓑ Ricky Rudd   Ⓓ Greg Biffle

9 Kansas Speedway also features a summer race from what *NASCAR* series?

Ⓐ NEXTEL Cup   Ⓒ Busch Series
Ⓑ Craftsman Truck Series Ⓓ NASCAR North

10 The 2001 race at Kansas Speedway was won by what driver?

Ⓐ Dale Earnhardt Jr.   Ⓒ Michael Waltrip
Ⓑ Jeff Gordon   Ⓓ Ricky Rudd

GETTING READY FOR
GREEN!

WORD SCRAMBLE

A C N R H
Drivers want to avoid
_____

G N E I N E
A car's power
_____

T P I O R A D
Where to go for gas or repairs (2 words)
_____

R H V O E L C T E
Both No. 8 and No. 24 are this
_____

N G E R E L A G F
It means go! (2 words)
_____

RACE #1

Date: _____

Race Name: _____

How's The Weather? _____

_____

_____

Pole Winner: _____

My driver's qualifying time and starting position were: _____

In the Pits: _____

_____

_____

My driver led _____ laps. There were _____ cautions.

My driver finished _____

_____ won the race.

My driver's point standings after the race: _____

_____

Who's the points leader now? _____

It was awesome when: _____

_____

_____

It was SO NOT COOL when: _____

_____

_____

I'll remember this race, because: _____

_____

_____

I went to the race with/watched it on TV with: _____

_____

We stayed at: _____

We had dinner at: _____

We tailgated and had: _____

New friends I met at the race are: _____

_____

What this race meant to me:

_____

_____

_____

_____

_____

_____

```
A T L A N T A D A E F A N
G E A R S H I F T H B G E
G A R A G E W E I G H T X
K B L O C K I N G C F I T
W U O J D R A F T I N G E
H M O L S Y M O S N T C L
E P S P C R N V Q U X H C
E Z E A U B W A L L W A U
L Y B E F L A G M A N S P
B D F G F L A G H I C S I
A K P A S S I N G J C I L
S O M P W H E E L B A S E
E N C O M P R E S S I O N
```

ATLANTA
AERODYNAMICS
BLOCKING
BUMP
CHASSIS
COMPRESSION
DRAFTING
FLAG
FLAGMAN
FSN
GARAGE
GEARSHIFT
LOOSE
NEXTEL CUP
PASSING
SCUFFS
WALL
WEIGHT
WHEELBASE

off the mark   by Mark Parisi
w w w . o f f t h e m a r k . c o m

©2004 MARK PARISI DIST. BY UFS, INC.
MarkParisi@aol.com
offthemark.com

NEW SAFETY UNDERWEAR WITH
WEDGIE-SENSITIVE AIRBAGS

©2000 Mark Parisi. Reprinted by permission.

LAS VEGAS
MOTOR SPEEDWAY

7000 LAS VEGAS BLVD. NORTH
LAS VEGAS, NEVADA

www.lvms.com

> "Stay out of trouble.
> The money is at the end of the race,
> not the beginning."
>
> —BUCK BAKER

It may seem like a dream, but **LAS VEGAS MOTOR SPEEDWAY** really does brings together the excitement of **NASCAR** with the non-stop action of Las Vegas.

It's big, it's fast, and there's plenty of room to get in trouble—and we're just talking about the race track!

Las Vegas and **NASCAR** are a marriage that could only happen in, well, Las Vegas. So get ready to hit the jackpot when the odds are for a great race at Las Vegas Motor Speedway!

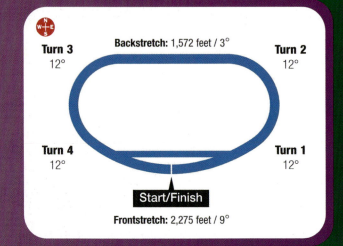

Turn 3
12°

Backstretch: 1,572 feet / 3°

Turn 2
12°

Turn 4
12°

Turn 1
12°

Start/Finish

Frontstretch: 2,275 feet / 9°

Pre-race advice

TrackFacts

Length:	1.5 Miles (267 laps = 400 miles)
Race Length:	400 Miles
Frontstretch:	2,275 feet/9°
Backstretch:	1,572 feet/3°
Grandstand Seating Capacity:	137,000
Banking:	All Turns—12°
First Race:	March 1, 1998—Las Vegas 400

On track action!

Qualifying & Race Records

Qualifying:	Bobby Labonte, Chevrolet, 173.016 mph (31.211 sec.); Feb. 28, 2003
Race:	Mark Martin, Ford, 146.554 mph (2:43:58); March 1, 1998
Most Wins:	2—Jeff Burton
Oldest Winner:	Sterling Marlin, 44 Years, 8 Months, 1 Day, March 3, 2002
Youngest Winner:	Jeff Gordon, 29 Years, 7 Months, March 4, 2001
Most Cautions:	6—Three times, most recently, March 2, 2003

TRIVIA

1. The winner of the 2004 UAW-Daimler Chrysler 400 at Las Vegas Motor Speedway was:

   A Kasey Kahne
   B Ryan Newman
   C Matt Kenseth
   D Greg Biffle

2. The turns at Las Vegas Motor Speedway are banked at:

   A 14 degrees
   B 12 degrees
   C 18 degrees
   D 36 degrees

3. The jackman:

   A Raises the car
   B Paints the car
   C Test drives the car
   D Fuels the car

4. The first **NASCAR** race at Las Vegas Motor Speedway was in:

   A 2001   B 2003   C 1998   D 1999

5. The winner of that race was?

   A Dale Earnhardt
   B Terry Labonte
   C Bobby Labonte
   D Mark Martin

6. The manufacturer with the most victories at Las Vegas Motor Speedway?

   A Dodge   B Ford   C Chevrolet   D Other

7. The winner of the 2003 UAW- Diamler Chrysler 400 was:

   A Kasey Kahne
   B Ryan Newman
   C Matt Kenseth
   D Greg Biffle

8. The window net:

   A Keeps the bugs out
   B Keeps driver's left arm inside the care
   C Transmits radio signals
   D Contributes to horsepower

9. **NASCAR** Cup Series cars have an automatic transmission:

   A True   B False

10. The fuel cell of a **NASCAR** Cup Series car is:

    A 10 gallons   B 14 gallons   C 42 gallons   D 22 gallons

THE FIELD HITS PIT ROAD

WORD SCRAMBLE

L A R I M N
Sterling

_____

S T O N I P I O
Where you stand

_____

P O L S I R E
Metal blade to regulate air flow

_____

H E C A I M N C
He works on the engine

_____

L D A L T A G E A
NASCAR'S biggest track

_____

RACE #1

Date: _____

Race Name: _____

How's The Weather? _____

_____

_____

Pole Winner: _____

My driver's qualifying time and starting position were: _____

In the Pits: _____

_____

_____

My driver led _____ laps. There were _____ cautions.

My driver finished _____

_____ won the race.

My driver's point standings after the race: _____

_____

Who's the points leader now? _____

It was awesome when: _____

_____

_____

It was SO NOT COOL when: _____

_____

_____

I'll remember this race, because: _____

_____

_____

I went to the race with/watched it on TV with:

_____

We stayed at: _____

We had dinner at: _____

We tailgated and had: _____

New friends I met at the race are: _____

_____

What this race meant to me:

_____

_____

_____

_____

_____

B	M	M	A	Y	F	I	E	L	D	Z	Y	A
F	D	A	F	E	P	N	N	F	G	P	H	N
I	A	T	C	J	U	N	I	O	R	E	H	D
T	D	T	I	X	A	U	J	Y	Y	T	A	R
T	B	S	W	R	C	R	X	T	K	T	Z	E
I	V	T	M	C	M	U	R	R	A	Y	Y	T
P	Q	L	P	G	G	R	E	E	N	M	W	T
A	B	U	R	T	O	N	N	V	T	Z	S	I
L	U	I	A	O	E	R	U	D	D	T	A	J
D	M	B	F	C	N	D	D	P	O	T	D	I
I	E	Q	L	F	K	R	L	O	N	G	L	F
R	I	G	G	S	L	A	B	O	N	T	E	H
F	S	K	A	H	N	E	G	M	E	A	R	S

ANDRETTI
BIFFLE
BURTON
FITTIPALDI
FOYT
GORDON
GREEN
JARRETT
JUNIOR
KAHNE
LABONTE
LONG
MATT
MAYFIELD
MCMURRAY
MEARS
PETTY
RIGGS
RUDD
SADLER

"I was watching the NASCAR race."

LOWE'S
MOTOR SPEEDWAY

5555 CONCORD PARKWAY SOUTH
CONCORD, NORTH CAROLINA

www.lowesmotorspeedway.com

> "You can live well or just live. And the person who makes that decision is you."
>
> —BOBBY ALLISON

Have you ever gotten really excited about going someplace, only to get there and find out that it is even *better* than you anticipated?

Well, get ready for , Charlotte's crown jewel of auto racing. Races at Lowe's Motor Speedway are like a home game for most of today's **NASCAR** drivers because they live in the area. Spending most of the year on the road can be a drag, so being able to hang with your buds at home is like a dream come true. Only, don't lay around dreaming too long because there's some heavy racing ahead at the one and half mile race track that invites lots of passing and some very fast racing.

NASCAR racing at Lowe's Motor Speedway . . . welcome home.

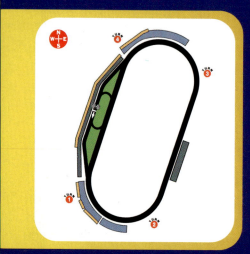

Night racing

TrackFacts

LENGTH: 1.5 Miles (400 laps = 600 miles or 334 laps = 500 miles)

RACE LENGTH: 600 Miles (1), 500 Miles (2)

FRONTSTRETCH: 1,952 feet/5°

BACKSTRETCH: 1,360 feet/5°

GRANDSTAND SEATING CAPACITY: 171,000

BANKING: All Turns—24°

FIRST RACE: June 19, 1960—World 600

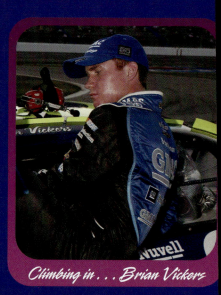

Climbing in . . . Brian Vickers

QUALIFYING & RACE RECORDS

QUALIFYING: Ryan Newman, Dodge, 186.657 mph (28.930 sec.); Oct. 9, 2003

RACE: 500 Miles—Jeff Gordon, Chevrolet, 160.306 mph (3:07:31); Oct. 11, 1999
600 Miles—Bobby Labonte, Pontiac, 151.952 (3:56:55); May 28, 1995

MOST WINS: 6—Bobby Allison and Darrell Waltrip

OLDEST WINNER: Cale Yarborough, 46 Years, 6 Months, 9 Days, Oct. 6, 1985

YOUNGEST WINNER: Jeff Gordon, 22 Years, 9 Months, 25 Days, May 29, 1994

MOST CAUTIONS: 14—May 25, 1980

TRIVIA

1. The winner of the 2004 Coca-Cola 600 at Lowe's Motor Speedway was:
   - **A** Brian Vickers
   - **B** Jimmie Johnson
   - **C** Kurt Busch
   - **D** Jeremy Mayfield

2. Lowe's Motor Speedway hosted its first **NASCAR** Cup Series race in:
   - **A** 1960
   - **B** 1971
   - **C** 2001
   - **D** 1952

3. The grandstand seating capacity at Lowe's Motor Speedway is:
   - **A** 1 Million
   - **B** 142,000
   - **C** 139,000
   - **D** 171,000

4. The turns at Lowe's Motor Speedway are banked:
   - **A** 14 degrees
   - **B** 36 degrees
   - **C** 24 degrees
   - **D** 18 degrees

5. The closest margin of victory at Lowe's Motor Speedway was 0.24 second. Who won and whom did he beat?
   - **A** Richard Petty over Bobby Allison in 1967
   - **B** Cale Yarborough over Benny Parsons in 1977
   - **C** Darrell Waltrip over Rusty Wallace in 1988
   - **D** Dale Jarrett over Jeff Gordon in 1996

6. The 2000 winner of the UAW-GM Quality 500 at Lowe's Motor Speedway was?
   - **A** Bobby Labonte
   - **B** Dale Jarrett
   - **C** Rusty Wallace
   - **D** Dale Earnhardt

7. What make of a car was he driving?
   - **A** Chevrolet
   - **B** Ford
   - **C** Pontiac
   - **D** Dodge

8. How many laps are the Coca-Cola 600 at Lowe's Motor Speedway?
   - **A** 600 laps
   - **B** 400 laps
   - **C** 267 laps
   - **D** 308 laps

9. Dale Earnhardt last won the Coca-Cola 600 at Lowe's Motor Speedway in what year?
   - **A** 1992
   - **B** 1999
   - **C** 1986
   - **D** 2000

10. Richard Petty won his last **NASCAR** Cup Series race at Lowe's Motor Speedway in what year?
    - **A** 1984
    - **B** 1983
    - **C** 1971
    - **D** 1978

BLINDING SPEED!

O Y R G E O
Drivers want to find it
_____

P A C N O H M I
The winner
_____

A R E C R A T C K
Where the events take place (2 words)
_____

H T G I T
The car is pushing out of a turn
_____

P D I N O A L N I S A I
Brickyard
_____

RACE #1

Date: _____

Race Name: _____

How's The Weather? _____

_____

_____

Pole Winner: _____

My driver's qualifying time and starting position were: _____

In the Pits: _____

_____

_____

My driver led _____ laps. There were _____ cautions.

My driver finished _____

_____ won the race.

My driver's point standings after the race: _____

_____

Who's the points leader now? _____

It was awesome when: _____

_____

_____

It was SO NOT COOL when: _____

_____

_____

I'll remember this race, because: _____

_____

_____

I went to the race with/watched it on TV with: _____

_____

We stayed at: _____

We had dinner at: _____

We tailgated and had: _____

New friends I met at the race are: _____

_____

What this race meant to me:

_____

_____

_____

_____

_____

RACE #2

Date: _____

Race Name: _____

How's The Weather? _____
_____
_____

Pole Winner: _____

My driver's qualifying time and starting position were: _____

In the Pits: _____
_____
_____

My driver led _____ laps. There were _____ cautions.

My driver finished _____

_____ won the race.

My driver's point standings after the race: _____
_____

Who's the points leader now? _____

It was awesome when: _____
_____
_____

It was SO NOT COOL when: _____
_____
_____

I'll remember this race, because: _____
_____
_____

I went to the race with/watched it on TV with:
_____

We stayed at: _____

We had dinner at: _____

We tailgated and had: _____

New friends I met at the race are: _____
_____

What this race meant to me:
_____
_____
_____
_____
_____
_____

MARTINSVILLE
SPEEDWAY

340 SPEEDWAY ROAD
MARTINSVILLE, VIRGINIA

www.martinsvillespeedway.com

> "Martinsville Speedway always has been my baby doll, and we'll always keep her beautiful."
> —CLAY EARLES, FOUNDER MARTINSVILLE SPEEDWAY

Anyone who tells you that all **NASCAR** is about is a bunch of cars racing around in a circle needs to wake up and smell the burning rubber at Martinsville. It just might be the place to shock them back into reality.

Martinsville is the smallest track in the **NASCAR** Series at .526-miles, but don't let the comfy confines fool you. **MARTINSVILLE SPEEDWAY** actually pre-dates **NASCAR** itself and its unique design has stood the test of time, annually producing a champion that knows how to work his car through the tight spots as well as others who know how to charge hard at the bigger tracks. Martinsville's not about pure muscle: it takes careful planning, strategy and luck to come out of this one on top.

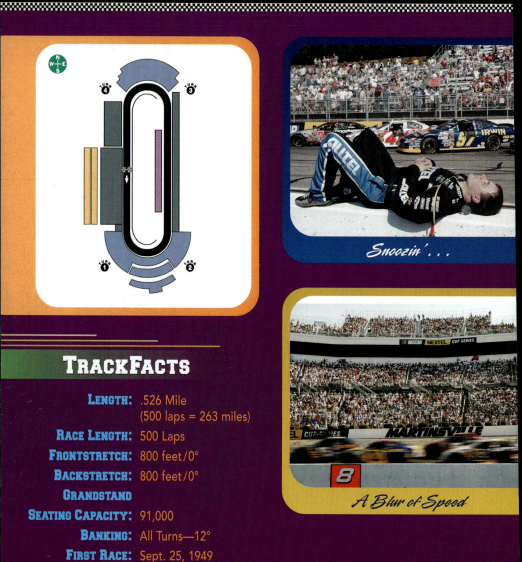

Snoozin'...

A Blur of Speed

TrackFacts

Length:	.526 Mile (500 laps = 263 miles)
Race Length:	500 Laps
Frontstretch:	800 feet/0°
Backstretch:	800 feet/0°
Grandstand Seating Capacity:	91,000
Banking:	All Turns—12°
First Race:	Sept. 25, 1949

Qualifying & Race Records

Qualifying:	Ryan Newman, Dodge, 97.043 mph (19.513 sec.); Oct. 24, 2004
Race:	Jeff Gordon, Chevrolet, 82.223 mph (3:11:55); Sept. 22, 1996
Most Wins:	15—Richard Petty
Oldest Winner:	Harry Gant, 51 Years, 8 Months, 12 Days, Sept. 22, 1991
Youngest Winner:	Richard Petty, 22 Years, 9 Months, 8 Days, April 10, 1960
Most Cautions:	18—Oct. 1, 2000

TRIVIA

1 Martinsville Speedway is located in what state?

A South Carolina   **C** Alabama   **B** North Carolina   **D** Virginia

2 Martinsville Speedway is:

A A Superspeedway   **C** *NASCAR'S* newest track
B The smallest track in *NASCAR*   **D** A road course

3 The winner of the 2004 Advance Auto Parts 500 at Martinsville Speedway was:

A Jimmie Johnson   **C** Rusty Wallace
B Mark Martin   **D** Ryan Newman

4 The driver with the most wins at Martinsville Speedway is:

A Richard Petty   **C** Dale Earnhardt
B Darrell Waltrip   **D** Morgan Shepard

5 How many wins did he have?

A 40 Wins   **B** 11 Wins   **C** 15 Wins   **D** 8 Wins

6 Who was the youngest winner at Martinsville Speedway at 22 years, 9 months, and 8 days?

A Kurt Busch   **C** Richard Petty   **B** Jeff Gordon   **D** Ricky Rudd

7 In 1996, who set the track race record in a 500 lap race of 3:11:55 at 82.223 mph?

A Ricky Rudd   **C** Dale Earnhardt
B Jeff Gordon   **D** Jeff Burton

8 The first *NASCAR* race held at Martinsville Speedway was what year?

A 1949   **B** 1971   **C** 1959   **D** 1962

9 Petty Enterprises is the car owner with the most wins at Martinsville Speedway, who is second?

A Junior Johnson   **C** Rick Hendrick
B Dale Earnhardt   **D** Holman-Moody

10 Who won both cup races at Martinsville Speedway in 1989?

A Bobby Hamilton   **C** Richard Petty   **B** Ernie Ervan   **D** Darrell Waltrip

WORD SCRAMBLE

L A R U H E

The team's base during a race

_____

M E H E L T

Critical for driver safety

_____

S L G F A

Wave them to signal drivers

_____

S E U N O S P S N I

The car rides on it

_____

O U P H O R R E S E

How much power an engine has

_____

CUP SERIES.

TRADING PAINT!

RACE #1

Date: _____

Race Name: _____

How's The Weather? _____

_____

Pole Winner: _____

My driver's qualifying time and starting position were: _____

In the Pits: _____

_____

_____

My driver led _____ laps. There were _____ cautions.

My driver finished _____

_____ won the race.

My driver's point standings after the race: _____

_____

Who's the points leader now? _____

It was awesome when: _____

_____

_____

It was SO NOT COOL when: _____

_____

_____

I'll remember this race, because: _____

_____

_____

I went to the race with/watched it on TV with: _____

_____

We stayed at: _____

We had dinner at: _____

We tailgated and had: _____

New friends I met at the race are: _____

_____

What this race meant to me: _____

_____

_____

_____

_____

_____

RACE #2

Date: _____

Race Name: _____

How's The Weather? _____
_____
_____

Pole Winner: _____

My driver's qualifying time and starting position were: _____

In the Pits: _____
_____
_____

My driver led _____ laps. There were _____ cautions.

My driver finished _____
_____ won the race.

My driver's point standings after the race: _____
_____

Who's the points leader now? _____

It was awesome when: _____
_____
_____

It was SO NOT COOL when: _____
_____
_____

I'll remember this race, because: _____
_____
_____

I went to the race with/watched it on TV with:
_____

We stayed at: _____

We had dinner at: _____

We tailgated and had: _____

New friends I met at the race are: _____
_____

What this race meant to me:
_____
_____
_____
_____
_____
_____

Family Memories and NASCAR

My grandfather was one of the most important people in my life, and he was the one who introduced me to NASCAR. When I was eleven he even took me to a race so I could see the real thing. When my grandfather was diagnosed with cancer he couldn't move around too much, so I would spend Saturday and Sunday with him cheering for our favorite drivers. Then on the following Monday, I would share with him every article I had found in our local newspaper or online about the race we had watched together. My grandfather would have me read the articles to him and then he would ask me if I agreed with what the writer said. He passed away last summer after a long battle with cancer, but even though he is gone my grandfather will live in my heart forever—especially whenever I think of NASCAR.   Austin

My father always went to NASCAR races with his friend. This year at the last second, his friend couldn't go due to a family illness and my dad asked me if I wanted to go. Even though I can't say I was a NASCAR fan, I was so excited that he had asked me and that I would be spending time with my dad— just the two of us—that I couldn't say yes fast enough. When we got to the race, the scene was almost overwhelming; the sounds of the cars and the power of their engines, the excitement, the colors, the fans— it was all awesome! I'll never forget that first race and now I'm a huge fan.   Jennifer

My family memories of NASCAR:

_____

_____

_____

_____

_____

NOTHING LIKE BEING THERE!

FAMILY TIME . . . NASCAR STYLE

MICHIGAN
INTERNATIONAL SPEEDWAY

12626 US HIGHWAY 121
BROOKLYN, MICHIGAN

www.mispeedway.com

> "I figure you get out of life just about what you put into it."
>
> —LEE PETTY

MICHIGAN INTERNATIONAL SPEEDWAY is a race car driver's race track. First of all, the track is just plain big. In fact, it is two miles long in a smooth D-shaped oval. Second, it's wide, giving drivers plenty of room to find their groove—high, low or in the middle. Finally, high banking and long straightaways provide the runways for these rockets to really fly.

If watching a *NASCAR* race car go flat out and show you all of its impressive power is your ideal race, then Michigan International Speedway is for you.

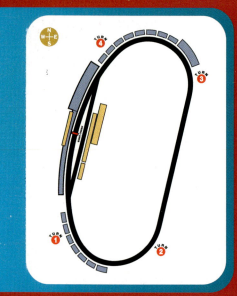

Coming Down The Frontstretch

TrackFacts

Length:	2 Miles (200 laps = 400 miles)
Race Length:	400 Miles (1), 400 Miles (2)
Frontstretch:	3,600 feet/12°
Backstretch:	2,242 feet/5°
Grandstand Seating Capacity:	136,373
Banking:	All Turns—18°
First Race:	June 15, 1969—Motor State 500

Setting Strategy

Qualifying & Race Records

Qualifying:	Dale Earnhardt Jr., Chevrolet, 191.149 mph (37.667 sec.); Aug. 18, 2000
Race:	Dale Jarrett, Ford, 173.997 mph (2:17:56); June 13, 1999
Most Wins:	9—David Pearson
Oldest Winner:	Harry Gant, 52 Years, 7 Months, 6 Days, Aug. 16, 1992
Youngest Winner:	Kurt Busch, 24 Years, 10 Months, 11 Days, June 15, 2003
Most Cautions:	9—Twice, most recently, June 15, 2003

TRIVIA

1 The winner of the 2004 DHL 400 at Michigan International Speedway was:

- **Ⓐ** Elliott Sadler
- **Ⓑ** Jimmie Johnson
- **Ⓒ** Ryan Newman
- **Ⓓ** Mark Martin

2 The winner of the 2004 GFS Marketplace 400 at Michigan International Speedway was:

- **Ⓐ** Greg Biffle
- **Ⓒ** Jeff Gordon
- **Ⓑ** Jimmie Johnson
- **Ⓓ** Kurt Busch

3 Michigan International Speedway is how long?

- **Ⓐ** 1.44 Miles
- **Ⓑ** 2.38 Miles
- **Ⓒ** 1.98 Miles
- **Ⓓ** 2.0 Miles

4 The turns at Michigan International Speedway are banked at:

- **Ⓐ** 14 Degrees
- **Ⓑ** 18 Degrees
- **Ⓒ** 36 Degrees
- **Ⓓ** 9 Degrees

5 Michigan International Speedway is located in what city?

- **Ⓐ** Queens
- **Ⓑ** Brooklyn
- **Ⓒ** Manhattan
- **Ⓓ** Bronx

6 On August 18, 2000 who set Michigan International Speedway's qualifying record at 191.149 mph?

- **Ⓐ** Dale Earnhardt
- **Ⓑ** Dale Earnhardt Jr.
- **Ⓒ** Jeff Gordon
- **Ⓓ** Bill Elliott

7 The driver with the most wins (9) at Michigan International Speedway is:

- **Ⓐ** Buddy Baker
- **Ⓑ** Cale Yarborough
- **Ⓒ** Dale Earnhardt
- **Ⓓ** David Person

8 What manufacturer has the most wins at Michigan International Speedway?

- **Ⓐ** Ford
- **Ⓑ** Pontiac
- **Ⓒ** Chevrolet
- **Ⓓ** Dodge

9 Who is the oldest winner at Michigan International Speedway at 52 years old?

- **Ⓐ** Bill Elliott
- **Ⓑ** Harry Gant
- **Ⓒ** Richard Petty
- **Ⓓ** Bobby Allison

10 The record for the fewest cautions at Michigan International Speedway is zero, on three occasions, what year was the most recent?

- **Ⓐ** 2004
- **Ⓑ** 1999
- **Ⓒ** 2001
- **Ⓓ** 1978

BATTLING FOR POSITION

WORD SCRAMBLE

L O P E

Starting from the front

_____

O P O R S N S

You must have them to fund a team

_____

E R V R D I S

Stars of the sport

_____

E T Y T P

Legendary name

_____

D U E N S Y A P E S E R P

2.5 miles or longer

_____

RACE #1

Date: _____

Race Name: _____

How's The Weather? _____

_____

_____

Pole Winner: _____

My driver's qualifying time and starting position were: _____

In the Pits: _____

_____

_____

My driver led _____ laps. There were _____ cautions.

My driver finished _____

_____ won the race.

My driver's point standings after the race: _____

_____

Who's the points leader now? _____

It was awesome when: _____

_____

_____

It was SO NOT COOL when: _____

_____

_____

I'll remember this race, because: _____

_____

_____

I went to the race with/watched it on TV with: _____

_____

We stayed at: _____

We had dinner at: _____

We tailgated and had: _____

New friends I met at the race are: _____

_____

What this race meant to me:

_____

_____

_____

_____

RACE #2

Date: _____

Race Name: _____

How's The Weather? _____
_____
_____

Pole Winner: _____

My driver's qualifying time and starting position were: _____

In the Pits: _____
_____
_____

My driver led _____ laps. There were _____ cautions.

My driver finished _____
_____ won the race.

My driver's point standings after the race: _____
_____

Who's the points leader now? _____

It was awesome when: _____
_____
_____

It was SO NOT COOL when: _____
_____
_____

I'll remember this race, because: _____
_____
_____

I went to the race with/watched it on TV with: _____
_____

We stayed at: _____

We had dinner at: _____

We tailgated and had: _____

New friends I met at the race are: _____
_____

What this race meant to me:
_____
_____
_____
_____
_____
_____

NEW HAMPSHIRE
INTERNATIONAL SPEEDWAY

1122 ROUTE 106 NORTH
LOUDON, NEW HAMPSHIRE

www.nhis.com

> "Look for ways to win, rather than expecting something to happen that will make you lose."
>
> BILLY WADE

In a region that is not commonly identified with the sport, **NEW HAMPSHIRE INTERNATIONAL SPEEDWAY** is a New England **NASCAR** fan's salvation. But looks can be deceiving! Just rock out with the nearly 100,000 fans who make the bi-annual pilgrimage to the beauty of New Hampshire to scream their brains out for their favorite driver.

New Hampshire International Speedway has a character all its own in a track that is expansive yet retains the characteristics of some of **NASCAR'S** smaller tracks when it comes to turns and passing.

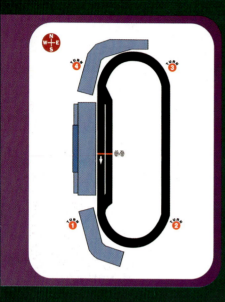

Passing!

TrackFacts

LENGTH: 1.058 Miles
(300 laps = 317.4 miles)

RACE LENGTH: 317.4 Miles (1), 317.4 Miles (2)

FRONTSTRETCH: 1,500 feet/2°

BACKSTRETCH: 1,500 feet/2°

GRANDSTAND
SEATING CAPACITY: 91,000

BANKING: All turns—12°

FIRST RACE: July 11, 1993—Slick 50 300

Restart

QUALIFYING & RACE RECORDS

QUALIFYING: Ryan Newman, Dodge, 133.357 mph (28.561 sec.); Sept. 12, 2003

RACE: Jeff Burton, Ford, 117.134 mph (2:42:35); July 13, 1997

MOST WINS: 4—Jeff Burton

OLDEST WINNER: Dale Jarrett, 44 Years, 7 Months, 26 Days, July 22, 2001

YOUNGEST WINNER: Jeff Gordon, 23 Years, 11 Months, 5 Days, July 9, 1995

MOST CAUTIONS: 17—July 10, 1994

TRIVIA

1 New Hampshire International Speedway is located in what part of the country?

Ⓐ Mid Atlantic   Ⓑ New England   Ⓒ Rocky Mountains   Ⓓ Midwest

2 **NASCAR** Cup's first race at New Hampshire International Speedway was what year?

Ⓐ 1978   Ⓑ 2002   Ⓒ 1999   Ⓓ 1993

3 The turns at New Hampshire International Speedway are banked:

Ⓐ 12 Degrees   Ⓑ 14 Degrees   Ⓒ 36 Degrees   Ⓓ 90 Degrees

4 The winner of the first **NASCAR** Cup race at New Hampshire International Speedway was won by:

Ⓐ Bill Elliott   Ⓑ Terry Labonte   Ⓒ Rusty Wallace   Ⓓ Dale Earnhardt

5 The winner at the 2004 Sylvania 300 at New Hampshire International Speedway was:

Ⓐ Jeremy Mayfield   Ⓒ Kurt Busch
Ⓑ Ryan Newman   Ⓓ Brian Vickers

6 The driver with the most wins at New Hampshire International Speedway is:

Ⓐ Richard Petty   Ⓒ Dale Earnhardt
Ⓑ Jeff Burton   Ⓓ Terry Labonte

7 As of 2003, the driver with the most top 10 finishes at New Hampshire International Speedway is:

Ⓐ Jeff Burton   Ⓑ Bobby Gordon   Ⓒ Jeff Gordon   Ⓓ Dale Jarrett

8 Name the oldest winner at 44 years and 7 months at New Hampshire International Speedway?

Ⓐ Dale Jarrett   Ⓑ Ward Burton   Ⓒ Joe Nemechek   Ⓓ Ernie Irvan

9 The manufacturer with the most wins (8) at New Hampshire International Speedway is:

Ⓐ Dodge   Ⓑ Pontiac   Ⓒ Chevrolet   Ⓓ Ford

10 Name the winner who holds the record for leading every lap?

Ⓐ Jeff Burton, 2000   Ⓒ Kurt Busch, 2004
Ⓑ Jimmie Johnson, 2003   Ⓓ Jeff Gordon, 1998

WORD SCRAMBLE

A N F

You

_____

E A R C M B

Tire tilt

_____

B H E L I S E A E

Distance between axles

_____

R I V N C K E

Brian

_____

S E I N C D T P A L E M

Cubic inch measurement of engine

_____

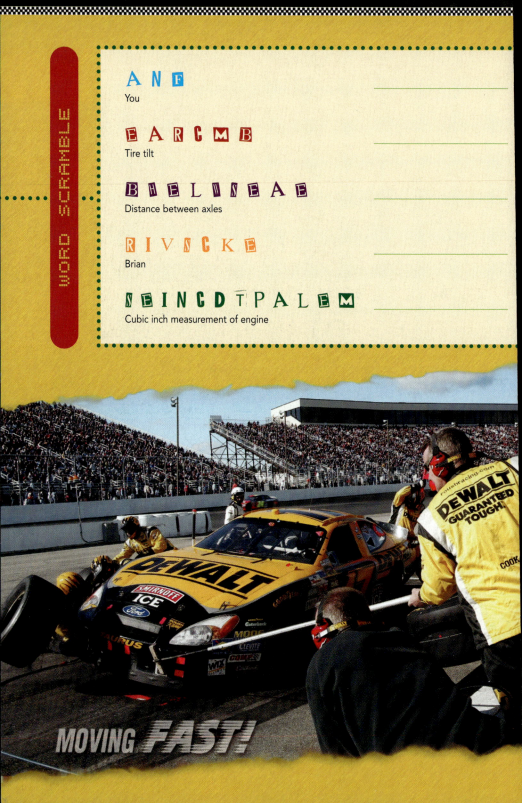

MOVING *FAST!*

RACE #1

Date: _____
Race Name: _____
How's The Weather? _____
_____
_____

Pole Winner: _____
My driver's qualifying time and starting position were: _____
_____

In the Pits: _____
_____
_____
My driver led _____ laps. There were _____ cautions.
My driver finished _____
_____ won the race.
My driver's point standings after the race: _____
_____
Who's the points leader now? _____

It was awesome when: _____
_____
_____
It was SO NOT COOL when: _____
_____
_____
I'll remember this race, because: _____
_____
_____

I went to the race with/watched it on TV with: _____
_____
We stayed at: _____
We had dinner at: _____
We tailgated and had: _____
New friends I met at the race are: _____
_____

What this race meant to me: _____
_____
_____
_____
_____
_____

RACE #2

Date: _____

Race Name: _____

How's The Weather? _____
_____
_____

Pole Winner: _____

My driver's qualifying time and starting position were: _____

In the Pits: _____
_____
_____

My driver led _____ laps. There were _____ cautions.

My driver finished _____
_____ won the race.

My driver's point standings after the race: _____
_____

Who's the points leader now? _____

It was awesome when: _____
_____
_____

It was SO NOT COOL when: _____
_____
_____

I'll remember this race, because: _____
_____
_____

I went to the race with/watched it on TV with: _____
_____

We stayed at: _____

We had dinner at: _____

We tailgated and had: _____

New friends I met at the race are: _____
_____

What this race meant to me:
_____
_____
_____
_____
_____
_____
_____

What I've learned about life from NASCAR

The biggest thing that NASCAR has taught me about life is that you can never give up. Whenever I am involved in something and I feel like quitting, I remember that over and over NASCAR drivers keep trying their best no matter what happens. Sometimes they win just by hanging in there!

Abe

Everyone cheers for their favorite driver, but it takes more than just the driver to win a race. NASCAR taught me that no matter what, you don't win anything by yourself. There are a lot of other people involved-look at all the pit stops! You have to work as a team to win-you can't do it alone.

Richie

Teamwork is important to me because . . .

_____
_____
_____
_____
_____
_____
_____
_____
_____
_____

TEAMWORK!

PHOENIX
INTERNATIONAL RACEWAY

7602 S. 115TH AVENUE
AVONDALE, ARIZONA

www.phoenixraceway.com

> "You've got to love this life.
> And I do."
>
> —J.D. MCDUFFIE, FORMER NASCAR DRIVER

If your idea of a good time is chilling by the pool, surrounded by some of the most beautiful scenery you have ever seen, all against the backdrop of big time *NASCAR* racing, then *PHOENIX INTERNATIONAL RACEWAY* is calling your name.

Phoenix is one of those places where everything always seems perfect: the weather, the setting and the racing. Phoenix International Raceway is a perfect reflection of its home because it is a modern, clean, accommodating racetrack that showcases great *(and fast)* racing that requires some careful thought and strategy in the turns.

So go ahead and take a dip, the water and the racing, are just about perfect.

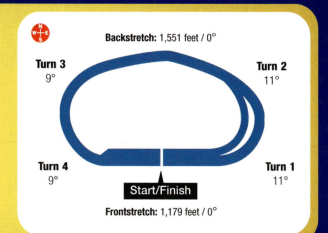

Backstretch: 1,551 feet / 0°

Turn 3
9°

Turn 2
11°

Turn 4
9°

Turn 1
11°

Start/Finish

Frontstretch: 1,179 feet / 0°

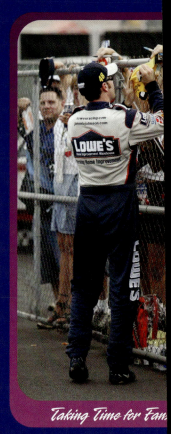

Taking Time for Fan...

TrackFacts

Length: 1 Mile (312 laps = 312 miles/500 kilometers)

Race Length: 500 Kilometers

Frontstretch: 1,179 feet / 0°

Backstretch: 1,551 feet / 0°

Grandstand Seating Capacity: 76,812

Banking: Turns 1 and 2—11°
Turns 3 and 4—9°

First Race: Nov. 6, 1988—Checker 500

Qualifying & Race Records

Qualifying: Rusty Wallace, Ford, 134.178 mph (26.830 sec.); Nov. 3, 2000

Race: Tony Stewart, Pontiac, 118.132 mph (2:38:28); Nov. 7, 1999

Most Wins: 2—Davey Allison and Jeff Burton

Oldest Winner: Rusty Wallace, 42 Years, 2 Months, 11 Days, Oct. 25, 1998

Youngest Winner: Tony Stewart, 28 Years, 5 Months, 18 Days, Nov. 7, 1999

Most Cautions: 10—Twice, most recently, Nov. 2, 2003

TRIVIA

1 Phoenix International Raceway is what shape?

A Square

C Tri-oval

B Circle

D D-shaped oval

2 The driver with the most top 10 finishes at Phoenix International Raceway is:

A Mark Martin (13)

C Dale Earnhardt (8)

B Davey Allison (4)

D Jeff Gordon (9)

3 A blue flag with a yellow stripe means:

A Yield to lap cars

C Pit road open

B One lap to go

D Stop

4 Joe Nemecheck's nickname is:

A Never Slow Joe

C Front Row Joe

B Way to Go Joe

D Prime Time Joe

5 Jeff Gordon's first start in the *NASCAR* Cup Series was:

A June 2001

C November 1992

B May 1996

D February 1994

6 Jeff Gordon drives a:

A Ford

B Chevrolet

C Dodge

D Other

7 Casey Mears' first full season in the *NASCAR* Cup Series was:

A 1971

B 2003

C 1999

D 1997

8 Kasey Kahne was born in what year?

A 1980

B 1976

C 1981

D 1979

9 The Chase for the *NASCAR* NEXTEL Cup Championship began in what year?

A 2002

B 1971

C 2004

D 1999

10 Turns 1 and 2, at 11 degrees are the same as turns 3 and 4 at Phoenix International Raceway?

A True, they are the same

B False, turns 3 and 4 are 9 degrees

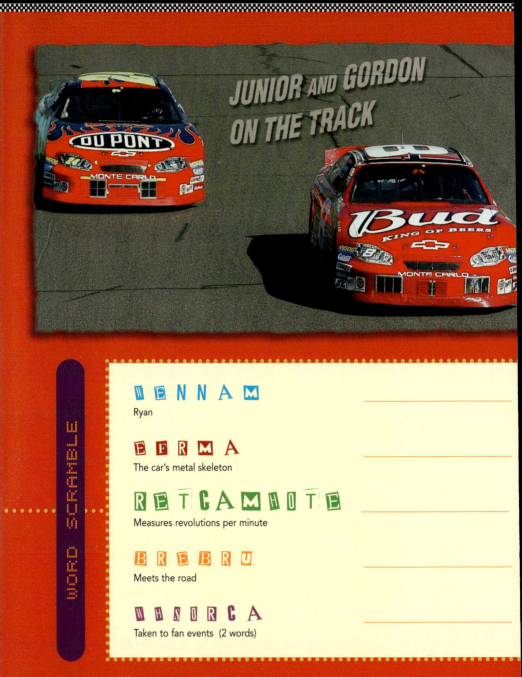

JUNIOR AND GORDON ON THE TRACK

NENNAM

Ryan

_____

EFRMA

The car's metal skeleton

_____

RETCAMHOTE

Measures revolutions per minute

_____

BREBRU

Meets the road

_____

WHSORCA

Taken to fan events (2 words)

_____

RACE #1

Date: _____
Race Name: _____
How's The Weather? _____
_____
_____

Pole Winner: _____
My driver's qualifying time and starting position were: _____
_____

In the Pits: _____
_____
_____
My driver led _____ laps. There were _____ cautions.
My driver finished _____
_____ won the race.
My driver's point standings after the race: _____
_____
Who's the points leader now? _____

It was awesome when: _____
_____
_____

It was SO NOT COOL when: _____
_____
_____

I'll remember this race, because: _____
_____
_____

I went to the race with/watched it on TV with: _____
_____

We stayed at: _____
We had dinner at: _____
We tailgated and had: _____
New friends I met at the race are: _____
_____

What this race meant to me: _____
_____
_____
_____
_____
_____

RACE #2

Date: _____

Race Name: _____

How's The Weather? _____

_____

_____

Pole Winner: _____

My driver's qualifying time and starting position were: _____

In the Pits: _____

_____

_____

My driver led _____ laps. There were _____ cautions.

My driver finished _____

_____ won the race.

My driver's point standings after the race: _____

_____

Who's the points leader now? _____

It was awesome when: _____

_____

_____

It was SO NOT COOL when: _____

_____

_____

I'll remember this race, because: _____

_____

_____

I went to the race with/watched it on TV with: _____

_____

We stayed at: _____

We had dinner at: _____

We tailgated and had: _____

New friends I met at the race are: _____

_____

What this race meant to me:

_____

_____

_____

_____

_____

_____

POCONO
RACEWAY

www.poconoraceway.com

> "Racing is like life. If you get up one more time than you fall, you'll make it through."
>
> —ALAN KULWICKI

Life is all about variety, right? Why, you never really know what will be coming at you next. In many ways life is a lot like *POCONO RACEWAY*.

It features a long, broad frontstretch that allows drivers to open it up and reach some flat out speeds of up to 200 mph, then it throws three distinctly styled turns, each one requiring its own unique style of circumvention.

Pocono is a track that requires a compromise between set up, aggression and strategy. Yea, that's a lot like life.

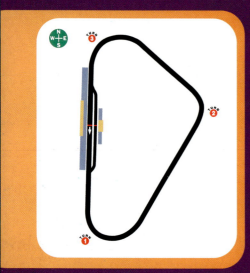

Heading to Pit Road

TrackFacts

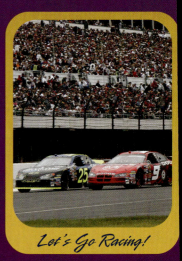

Length:	2.5 Miles (200 laps = 500 miles)
Race Length:	500 Miles (1), 500 Miles (2)
Frontstretch:	3,740 feet
Shortstretch:	1,780 feet
Backstretch:	3,055 feet
Grandstand Seating Capacity:	75,000
Banking:	Turn 1—14° • Turn 2—8° • Turn 3—6°
First Race:	Aug. 5, 1974—Purolator 500

Let's Go Racing!

Qualifying & Race Records

Qualifying:	Tony Stewart, Pontiac, 172.391 mph (52.207 sec.); July 21, 2000
Race:	Rusty Wallace, Ford, 144.892 mph (3:27:03); July 21, 1996
Most Wins:	5—Bill Elliott
Oldest Winner:	Harry Gant, 50 Years, 5 Months, 7 Days, June 17, 1990
Youngest Winner:	Jeff Gordon, 24 Years, 10 Months, 12 Days, June 16, 1996
Most Cautions:	13—June 17, 1990

TRIVIA

1 Turn 2 at Pocono Raceway is known as:

    Ⓐ Devil's Curve   **Ⓑ** Single File   **Ⓒ** Tunnel Turn   **Ⓓ** Shorty

2 The winner of the first *NASCAR* Cup Series race held at Pocono Raceway in 1974 was:

    Ⓐ David Person   **Ⓑ** Richard Petty   **Ⓒ** Darrell Waltrip   **Ⓓ** Benny Parsons

3 The driver with the most top 10 finishes at Pocono Raceway is:

    Ⓐ Tim Richmond (8)   **Ⓒ** Jeff Gordon (12)

    Ⓑ Dale Earnhardt (18)   **Ⓓ** Mark Martin (24)

4 Ryan Newman's hometown is:

    Ⓐ South Bend, Indiana   **Ⓒ** Indianapolis, Indiana

    Ⓑ Charlotte, North Carolina   **Ⓓ** Daytona Beach, Florida

5 The 2003 champion crew chief was:

    Ⓐ Robbie Reiser   **Ⓒ** Robbie Loomis

    Ⓑ Ray Everham   **Ⓓ** Jimmy Maker

6 Who is he the crew chief for?

    Ⓐ Jeff Gordon   **Ⓒ** Tony Stewart

    Ⓑ Dale Earnhardt   **Ⓓ** Matt Kenseth

7 The winner of the 2004 Pocono 500 was?

    Ⓐ Kasey Kahne   **Ⓒ** Ryan Newman

    Ⓑ Jimmie Johnson   **Ⓓ** Tony Stewart

8 The length of Pocono Raceway is:

    Ⓐ 1.99 Miles   **Ⓑ** 2.41 Miles   **Ⓒ** 2.5 Miles   **Ⓓ** 3.2 Miles

9 The manufacturer with the most wins (20) at Pocono Raceway is:

    Ⓐ Chevrolet   **Ⓑ** Buick   **Ⓒ** Saab   **Ⓓ** Ford

10 The July 30, 1978 race at Pocono Raceway featured the fewest cautions, how many were there?

    Ⓐ 0   **Ⓑ** 1   **Ⓒ** 8   **Ⓓ** 3

I R A L F N O

You drive through it (2 words)

_____

V E S N E

Number of crew members allowed over the wall

_____

U F L E   I M E L G A E

How far you can get on a tank of gas (2 words)

_____

S X E H U A T

Comes out of tail pipe

_____

R T S E E N I G

Determines cars direction

_____

RACE #1

Date: _____
Race Name: _____
How's The Weather? _____
_____
_____

Pole Winner: _____
My driver's qualifying time and starting position were: _____

In the Pits: _____
_____
_____
My driver led _____ laps. There were _____ cautions.
My driver finished _____
_____ won the race.
My driver's point standings after the race: _____
_____
Who's the points leader now? _____

It was awesome when: _____
_____
_____

It was SO NOT COOL when: _____
_____
_____

I'll remember this race, because: _____
_____
_____

I went to the race with/watched it on TV with: _____
_____
We stayed at: _____
We had dinner at: _____
We tailgated and had: _____
New friends I met at the race are: _____
_____

What this race meant to me:
_____
_____
_____
_____
_____
_____

RACE #2

Pole Winner: _____

My driver's qualifying time and starting position were: _____

Date: _____

Race Name: _____

How's The Weather? _____

_____

_____

In the Pits: _____

_____

_____

My driver led _____ laps. There were _____ cautions.

My driver finished _____

_____ won the race.

My driver's point standings after the race: _____

_____

Who's the points leader now? _____

It was awesome when: _____

_____

_____

It was SO NOT COOL when: _____

_____

_____

I'll remember this race, because: _____

_____

_____

I went to the race with/watched it on TV with: _____

_____

We stayed at: _____

We had dinner at: _____

We tailgated and had: _____

New friends I met at the race are: _____

_____

What this race meant to me:

_____

_____

_____

_____

_____

_____

I love NASCAR because...

I love NASCAR because it helps me have something to share with my dad. I only get to see him on weekends and there is nothing better than watching the race together—even though he is a fan of Junior and I like Jeff Gordon. Go 24!

Thomas

I like NASCAR because I feel like I know the drivers so well that they are, like, one of my friends or part of my family. You should hear the way everyone in my family yells at the drivers during a race, "Kurt, watch out!", "Don't let him pass, Mark," "Go Elliott, go!" You would think they can actually hear us!

Fritz

I love NASCAR because the drivers are cool and it's the only time our family watches TV in the same room at the same time without fighting!

Sissy

I love NASCAR because...

_____

_____

_____

_____

_____

_____

_____

_____

CELEBRATE!

VICTORY!

SPLASH!

RICHMOND
INTERNATIONAL RACEWAY

602 E. LABURNUM AVENUE
RICHMOND, VIRGINIA

www.rir.com

> "There's a lot of work and heartache to make it from the bottom to the top."
>
> —DAVID PEARSON

Sometimes less really is more. **RICHMOND INTERNATIONAL RACEWAY** measures only .750 miles but don't be fooled by its small size. Richmond is generally regarded as the drivers' favorite short track in the **NASCAR** Cup Series.

Race car drivers like to, well, race and Richmond International Raceway, in spite of its measurements, allows the drivers to do what they do relatively freely. You can race high, low or in the middle and the track is wide enough to let drivers pass where, and when, they feel like it. All this adds up to some exciting racing and, when the lights come on at night, it kicks it up another notch.

Night Racing

TRACKFACTS

LENGTH:	.75 Mile (400 laps = 300 miles)
RACE LENGTH:	Race Length: 400 Laps (1), 400 Laps (2)
FRONTSTRETCH:	1,290 feet/8°
BACKSTRETCH:	860 feet/2°
GRANDSTAND SEATING CAPACITY:	107,097
BANKING:	All turns—14°
FIRST RACE:	April 19, 1953—Richmond 200

Joking Around Before The Race

QUALIFYING & RACE RECORDS

QUALIFYING:	Ward Burton, Dodge, 127.389 mph (21.195 sec.); May 4, 2002
RACE:	Dale Jarrett, Ford, 109.047 mph (2:45:04); Sept. 6, 1997
MOST WINS:	13—Richard Petty
OLDEST WINNER:	Harry Gant, 51 Years, 7 Months, 28 Days, Sept. 7, 1991
YOUNGEST WINNER:	Richard Petty, 23 Years, 9 Months, 21 Days, April 23, 1961
MOST CAUTIONS:	15—May 3, 2003

TRIVIA

1. Richmond International Raceway is located in what state?
   - **A** South Carolina
   - **B** New Hampshire
   - **C** Delaware
   - **D** Virginia

2. The winner of the 2004 Chevy American Revolution 400 (May) at Richmond International Raceway was:
   - **A** Kasey Kahne
   - **B** Dale Earnhardt Jr.
   - **C** Rusty Wallace
   - **D** Ryan Newman

3. How long is Richmond International Raceway?
   - **A** 2.44 Miles
   - **B** 1.48 Miles
   - **C** .75 Mile
   - **D** 1.12 Miles

4. Richard Petty won how many **NASCAR** Cup Series races?
   - **A** 175
   - **B** 98
   - **C** 104
   - **D** 200

5. The winner of the 2004 Chevy Rock and Roll 400 (September) at Richmond International Raceway was:
   - **A** Jeremy Mayfield
   - **B** Tony Stewart
   - **C** Jimmie Johnson
   - **D** Kurt Busch

6. Which driver has the most starts of all time at 1,177?
   - **A** Richard Petty
   - **B** Dale Earnhardt
   - **C** David Pearson
   - **D** Buck Baker

7. In 1998, who won four events in a row?
   - **A** Dale Earnhardt
   - **B** Mark Martin
   - **C** Jeff Gordon
   - **D** Terry Labonte

8. When was the first race at Richmond International Raceway?
   - **A** June 1, 1938
   - **B** April 19, 1953
   - **C** March 31, 1961
   - **D** February 30, 1971

9. In 2003, who was the driver who lead the most laps (1,509.12)?
   - **A** Jeff Gordon
   - **B** Ryan Newman
   - **C** Tony Stewart
   - **D** Matt Kenseth

10. What manufacturer has the most wins (27) at Richmond International Raceway?
    - **A** Ford
    - **B** Pontiac
    - **C** Tie, Chevrolet & Ford
    - **D** Chevrolet

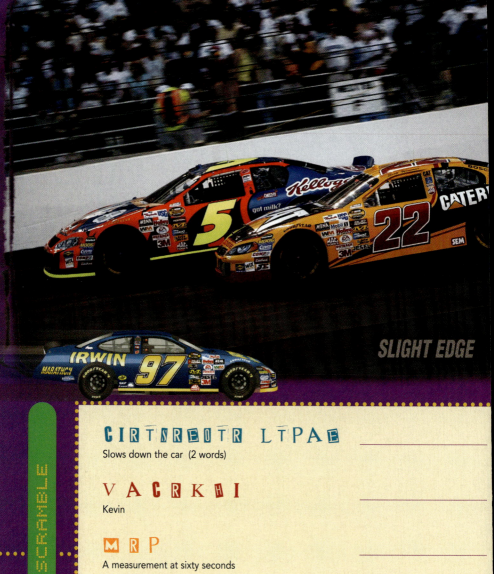

SLIGHT EDGE

WORD SCRAMBLE

CIRTSREOTR LTPAE _____
Slows down the car (2 words)

VACRKHI _____
Kevin

MRP _____
A measurement at sixty seconds

URDF _____
Kurt Busch drives one

RUGTPAAOH _____
You ask a driver for one

RACE #1

Date: _____

Race Name: _____

How's The Weather? _____

_____

_____

Pole Winner: _____

My driver's qualifying time and starting position were: _____

In the Pits: _____

_____

_____

My driver led _____ laps. There were _____ cautions.

My driver finished _____

_____ won the race.

My driver's point standings after the race: _____

_____

Who's the points leader now? _____

It was awesome when: _____

_____

_____

It was SO NOT COOL when: _____

_____

_____

I'll remember this race, because: _____

_____

_____

I went to the race with/watched it on TV with: _____

_____

We stayed at: _____

We had dinner at: _____

We tailgated and had: _____

New friends I met at the race are: _____

_____

What this race meant to me:

_____

_____

_____

_____

_____

RACE #2

Date: _____
Race Name: _____
How's The Weather? _____
_____
_____

Pole Winner: _____
My driver's qualifying time and starting position were: _____

In the Pits: _____
_____
_____
My driver led _____ laps. There were _____ cautions.
My driver finished _____
_____ won the race.
My driver's point standings after the race: _____
_____
Who's the points leader now? _____

It was awesome when: _____
_____
_____
It was SO NOT COOL when: _____
_____
_____
I'll remember this race, because: _____
_____
_____

I went to the race with/watched it on TV with: _____
_____
We stayed at: _____
We had dinner at: _____
We tailgated and had: _____
New friends I met at the race are: _____
_____

What this race meant to me:
_____
_____
_____
_____
_____
_____

TALLADEGA
SUPERSPEEDWAY

3366 SPEEDWAY BOULEVARD
TALLADEGA, ALABAMA

www.talladegasuperspeedway.com

"This is my place."

—DALE EARNHARDT JR.

The name says it all, *TALLADEGA SUPERSPEEDWAY*. And man, do they mean it.

Talladega is the longest track in **NASCAR** and it is *all business*. Come here ready to race. It measures 2.66 miles *(slightly larger than Daytona International Speedway)* in a tri-oval shape. Oh yea, Talladega is fast and big, with a generous track that often features cars charging four *(or more)* wide as they rip down the frontstretch.

It's not a track for the timid and its reputation continues to grow: with the 2004 EA Sports 500, Dale Earnhardt Jr. now owns five victories at Talladega and trails only his legendary father, Dale Earnhardt, who won here ten times.

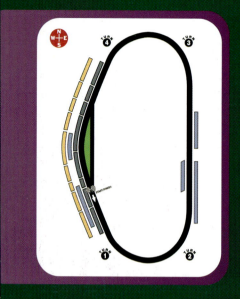

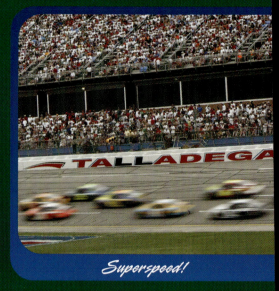

Superspeed!

TrackFacts

LENGTH:	2.66 Miles (188 laps = 500 miles)
RACE LENGTH:	500 Miles (1), 500 Miles (2)
FRONTSTRETCH:	4,300 feet/18°
BACKSTRETCH:	4,000 feet/2°
GRANDSTAND SEATING CAPACITY:	143,000
BANKING:	All turns—33°
FIRST RACE:	Sept. 14, 1969—Talladega 500

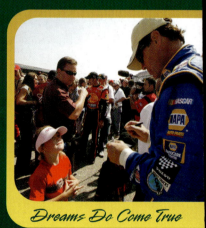

Dreams Do Come True

Qualifying & Race Records

QUALIFYING:	Bill Elliott, Ford, 212.809 mph (44.998 sec.); April 30, 1987
RACE:	Mark Martin, Ford, 188.354 mph (2:39:18); May 10, 1997
MOST WINS:	10—Dale Earnhardt
OLDEST WINNER:	Harry Gant, 51 Years, 3 Months, 26 Days, May 6, 1991
YOUNGEST WINNER:	Bobby Hillin Jr., 22 Years, 1 Month, 22 Days, July 27, 1986
MOST CAUTIONS:	9—Four times, most recently, May 3, 1987

1 What is the length of Talladega Superspeedway?

Ⓐ 2.66 Miles   **Ⓑ** 2.44 Miles   **Ⓒ** 1.99 Miles   **Ⓓ** 3.0 Miles

2 What driver, with 10, has won the most races at Talladega Superspeedway?

Ⓐ Dale Earnhardt Jr.   **Ⓒ** Dale Earnhardt

Ⓑ Richard Petty   **Ⓓ** Jeff Gordon

3 As of the start of the 2003 season, the current driver with the most starts, a total of 803, is:

Ⓐ Ricky Rudd   **Ⓒ** Kyle Petty

Ⓑ Terry Labonte   **Ⓓ** Mark Martin

4 How many people can the grandstand hold at Talladega Superspeedway?

Ⓐ 143,000   **Ⓑ** 168,000   **Ⓒ** 96,500   **Ⓓ** 75,000

5 The turns are banked at:

Ⓐ 14 degrees   **Ⓒ** 33 degrees

Ⓑ 21 degrees   **Ⓓ** 26 degrees

6 Darrell Waltrip won how many *NASCAR* Cup Series races?

Ⓐ 24   **Ⓑ** 84   **Ⓒ** 50   **Ⓓ** 60

7 With 126 poles, what driver is the all-time pole winner?

Ⓐ Richard Petty   **Ⓒ** Darrell Waltrip

Ⓑ David Pearson   **Ⓓ** Bobby Allison

8 Michael McSwain is crew chief for:

Ⓐ Bobby Labonte   **Ⓒ** Jeff Green

Ⓑ Kevin Harvick   **Ⓓ** Ricky Rudd

9 The driver with the second most wins, five, at Talladega Superpeedway is:

Ⓐ Richard Petty   **Ⓒ** Dale Earnhardt Jr.

Ⓑ Jeff Gordon   **Ⓓ** Darrell Waltrip

10 The EA Sports 500 at Talladega Superspeedway is how many laps?

Ⓐ 500 laps   **Ⓑ** 300 laps   **Ⓒ** 198 laps   **Ⓓ** 188 laps

WORD SCRAMBLE

R K C E H E E D C G F L A
_____
You've Won! (2 words)

I N B K A G N
_____
Degree of slant

I A L R N T P
_____
Racing brothers

L R L O   R B A
_____
Part of car's frame (2 words)

U M C M R A Y R
_____
Young star

RACING FOUR WIDE!

RACE #1

Date: _____
Race Name: _____
How's The Weather? _____
_____
_____

Pole Winner: _____
My driver's qualifying time and starting position were: _____
_____

In the Pits: _____
_____
_____
My driver led _____ laps. There were _____ cautions.
My driver finished _____
_____ won the race.
My driver's point standings after the race: _____
_____
Who's the points leader now? _____

It was awesome when: _____
_____
_____

It was SO NOT COOL when: _____
_____
_____

I'll remember this race, because: _____
_____
_____

I went to the race with/watched it on TV with: _____
_____

We stayed at: _____
We had dinner at: _____
We tailgated and had: _____
New friends I met at the race are: _____
_____

What this race meant to me:
_____
_____
_____
_____
_____

RACE #2

Date: _____

Race Name: _____

How's The Weather? _____
_____
_____

Pole Winner: _____

My driver's qualifying time and starting position were: _____

In the Pits: _____
_____
_____

My driver led _____ laps. There were _____ cautions.

My driver finished _____
_____ won the race.

My driver's point standings after the race: _____
_____

Who's the points leader now? _____

It was awesome when: _____
_____
_____

It was SO NOT COOL when: _____
_____
_____

I'll remember this race, because: _____
_____
_____

I went to the race with/watched it on TV with: _____
_____

We stayed at: _____

We had dinner at: _____

We tailgated and had: _____

New friends I met at the race are: _____
_____

What this race meant to me:
_____
_____
_____
_____
_____
_____

If I could spend a day with . . .

My dream would be answered if I could hang out for the day with Kasey Kahne. I would bring him to my school so that he could meet all my friends. Maybe he could bring his car with him, and show us up close how it works. Then we would play video games together.

Ben

I'd like to hang out with Dale Earnhardt Jr. I would want him to be himself and not have to act differently because I am around him. I would want to make him comfortable. So we'd hang out with his friends in his hometown, or visit his house.

LuLu

My friends know that I am so in love with Kasey Kahne and I would just die to meet him! If I got to hang out with Kasey for a day I would have a blast while we rode around in his No. 9 car. After that, I would show Kasey off to all my classmates and my friends. When we were done hanging with my friends, I would show him around my hometown. Then I would ask him if I could meet some of the other drivers too.

Ayla

If I could spend the day with . . .

_____

_____

_____

_____

_____

_____

_____

_____

CHILLIN'

HANGIN'
WITH
KASEY

TEXAS
MOTOR SPEEDWAY

3601 HIGHWAY 114
JUSTIN, TEXAS

www.texasmotorspeedway.com

> "There's no reason NOT
> to aim high."
>
> —HARRY GANT

TEXAS MOTOR SPEEDWAY is part of the modern **NASCAR** track family that just seems to have it all: a broad, fun race track that the drivers really like and all of the fun stuff that fans need to make a trip to the track one to remember.

NASCAR is skyrocketing in popularity and tracks like Texas Motor Speedway are a big part of the reason why. When you get there you feel like you are home and you never want to leave. They have done everything you can think of to make the track comfortable and friendly. The only part about a trip to the Texas Motor Speedway that could possibly be better was if you were actually *in* the race!

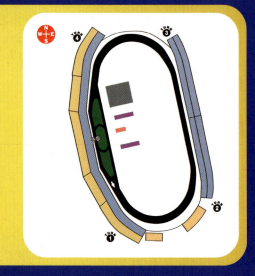

No. 15 Pit Stop

Photo Finish!

TrackFacts

LENGTH:	1.5 Miles (334 laps = 501 miles)
RACE LENGTH:	500 Miles (1)
FRONTSTRETCH:	2,250 feet/5°
BACKSTRETCH:	1,330 feet/5°
GRANDSTAND SEATING CAPACITY:	154,861
BANKING:	All Turns—24°
FIRST RACE:	April 6, 1997—Interstate Batteries 500

Qualifying & Race Records

QUALIFYING:	Bill Elliott, Dodge, 194.224 mph (27.803 sec.); April 5, 2002
RACE:	Terry Labonte, Chevrolet, 144.276 mph (3:28:21); Mar. 28, 1999
MOST WINS:	1—Jeff Burton, Dale Earnhardt Jr., Dale Jarrett, Matt Kenseth, Terry Labonte, Mark Martin, Ryan Newman and Elliott Sadler
OLDEST WINNER:	Dale Jarrett, 44 Years, 4 Months, 6 Days, April 1, 2001
YOUNGEST WINNER:	Ryan Newman, 25 Years, 3 Months, 22 Days, March 30, 2003
MOST CAUTIONS:	12—April 2, 2000

TRIVIA

1 The winner of the 2004 Samsung/Radio Shack 500 (April) at Texas Motor Speedway?

A. Greg Biffle   B. Kurt Busch   C. Elliott Sadler   D. Tony Stewart

2 Who has the record for winning at least one **NASCAR** Cup Series pole for twenty straight years?

A. Richard Petty (1965–1985)   C. Dale Earnhardt (1979–1999)

B. David Pearson (1963–1983)   D. Bill Elliott (1983–2003)

3 Bobby Allison won how many **NASCAR** Cup Series races?

A. 69   B. 84   C. 91   D. 102

4 The length of Texas Motor Speedway is?

A. 1.5 Miles   B. 2.3 Miles   C. 1.95 Miles   D. 2.0 Miles

5 The first race at Texas Motor Speedway was held in what year?

A. 1977   B. 1967   C. 1997   D. 1987

6 The oldest winner, at 44 years, 4 months, at Texas Motor Speedway is?

A. Dale Jarrett   C. Rusty Wallace

B. Ricky Rudd   D. Dale Earnhardt

7 The winner of the first race at Texas Motor Speedway was?

A. Richard Petty   C. Junior Johnson

B. Jeff Burton   D. Darrell Waltrip

8 Cale Yarborough won how many **NASCAR** Cup Series races?

A. 24   B. 14   C. 83   D. 60

9 The **NASCAR NEXTEL** All-Star Challenge is held at what track?

A. Daytona International Speedway   C. Texas Motor Speedway

B. Lowe's Motor Speedway   D. Atlanta Motor Speedway

10 The car owner with the most wins at Texas Motor Speedway is:

A. Jack Roush   C. Roger Penske

B. Rick Hendrick   D. Robert Yates

LINING UP!

O U S N C O

Official fuel

_____

K A G S T E

Seals engine parts

_____

N I P S T O

Works with cylinder in inner engine

_____

T F O Y

A.J.

_____

E F I N I D L

Middle of the track

_____

RACE #1

Date: _____
Race Name: _____
How's The Weather? _____
_____
_____

Pole Winner: _____
My driver's qualifying time and starting position were: _____
_____

In the Pits: _____
_____
_____

My driver led _____ laps. There were _____ cautions.
My driver finished _____
_____ won the race.
My driver's point standings after the race: _____
_____
Who's the points leader now? _____

It was awesome when: _____
_____
_____

It was SO NOT COOL when: _____
_____
_____

I'll remember this race, because: _____
_____
_____

I went to the race with/watched it on TV with: _____
_____
We stayed at: _____
We had dinner at: _____
We tailgated and had: _____
New friends I met at the race are: _____
_____

What this race meant to me:
_____
_____
_____
_____
_____

RACE #2

Date: _____

Race Name: _____

How's The Weather? _____
_____
_____

Pole Winner: _____

My driver's qualifying time and starting position were: _____

In the Pits: _____
_____
_____

My driver led _____ laps. There were _____ cautions.

My driver finished _____
_____ won the race.

My driver's point standings after the race: _____
_____

Who's the points leader now? _____

It was awesome when: _____
_____
_____

It was SO NOT COOL when: _____
_____
_____

I'll remember this race, because: _____
_____
_____

I went to the race with/watched it on TV with: _____
_____

We stayed at: _____

We had dinner at: _____

We tailgated and had: _____

New friends I met at the race are: _____
_____

What this race meant to me:
_____
_____
_____
_____
_____

WATKINS GLEN
INTERNATIONAL

2790 COUNTY ROUTE 16
WATKINS GLEN, NEW YORK

www.theglen.com

> "Winners never quit and quitters never win. It's true in life. It's true on the track."
>
> —BILL FRANCE JR.

WATKINS GLEN INTERNATIONAL is another cool example of how **NASCAR** likes to keep things *really* interesting.

Watkins Glen, or just "the Glen," as it is commonly known, is a road course just like Infineon Raceway, only it has some distinctive characteristics. The Glen stretches out over 2.45 miles and features tons of turns in every conceivable shape and size, both left and right, with enough room for drivers to open it up. All of this adds up to one of **NASCAR** Series' most unique racing experiences because you get to watch the drivers deal with the challenges of road racing while still kickin' it in where they can.

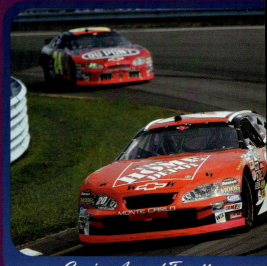

Coming Around Turn 11

TRACKFACTS

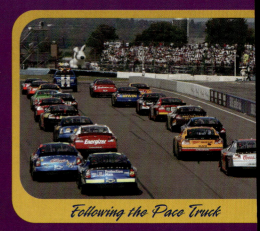

Following the Pace Truck

LENGTH: 2.45 Miles
(90 laps = 220.5 miles)

RACE LENGTH: 90 Laps

FRONTSTRETCH: N/A

BACKSTRETCH: N/A

GRANDSTAND SEATING CAPACITY: N/A

BANKING: 11 Turns

FIRST RACE: Aug. 4, 1957—The Glen

QUALIFYING & RACE RECORDS

QUALIFYING: Jeff Gordon, Chevrolet, 124.580 mph (70.798 sec.); Aug. 8, 2003

RACE: Mark Martin, Ford, 103.300 mph (2:11:54); Aug. 13, 1995

MOST WINS: 4—Jeff Gordon

OLDEST WINNER: Geoffrey Bodine, 47 Years, 3 Months, 24 Days, Aug. 11, 1996

YOUNGEST WINNER: Jeff Gordon, 26 Years, 6 Days, Aug. 10, 1997

MOST CAUTIONS: 8—Aug. 14, 1988

TRIVIA

1 Watkins Glen International is a:

A D-Shaped oval

B Tri-oval

C Road Course

D Egg shaped oval

2 The winner of the 2004 Sirius at The Glen was:

A Jimmie Johnson

B Tony Stewart

C Dale Earnhardt Jr.

D Kasey Kahne

3 How long is Watkins Glen International?

A 2.45 Miles   **B** 2.12 Miles   **C** 1.99 Miles   **D** 2.05 Miles

4 The driver with the most wins at Watkins Glen International is?

A Mark Martin (3)

B Jeff Gordon (4)

C Rusty Wallace (2)

D Richard Petty (25)

5 The car owner with the most wins (6) at Watkins Glen International is:

A Jack Roush   **B** Rick Hendrick   **C** Buck Baker   **D** Joe Gibbs

6 In 1998, he scored his first win in the *NASCAR* Cup Series.

A Jeff Burton

B Tony Stewart

C Jeremy Mayfield

D John Andretti

7 Michael Waltrip was born in what year?

A 1963   **B** 1980   **C** 1969   **D** 1959

8 In 1996, with three races to go, Jeff Gordon led this driver by only three points for the *NASCAR* Cup Series Championship?

A Dale Earnhardt   **B** Bill Elliott   **C** Terry Labonte   **D** Ricky Rudd

9 This driver competed from 1972 to 2000, winning 84 races and 3 *NASCAR* Cup Series Championship titles. Who is he?

A Bobby Allison

B Darrell Waltrip

C Benny Parsons

D Cale Yarborough

10 Watkins Glen International is in what state?

A New York   **B** South Carolina   **C** Alabama   **D** Virginia

WORD SCRAMBLE

C U B S H
Kurt
_____

N A N B N I G
A track's slope
_____

A T T U S R E
Tony
_____

N A L I D U G N
How a car feels
_____

U E K I R U
First year
_____

*WORKING
THROUGH
THE FIELD*

RACE #1

Date: _____

Race Name: _____

How's The Weather? _____

_____

_____

Pole Winner: _____

My driver's qualifying time and starting position were: _____

In the Pits: _____

_____

_____

My driver led _____ laps. There were _____ cautions.

My driver finished _____

_____ won the race.

My driver's point standings after the race: _____

_____

Who's the points leader now? _____

It was awesome when: _____

_____

_____

It was SO NOT COOL when: _____

_____

_____

I'll remember this race, because: _____

_____

_____

I went to the race with/watched it on TV with: _____

_____

We stayed at: _____

We had dinner at: _____

We tailgated and had: _____

New friends I met at the race are: _____

_____

What this race meant to me:

_____

_____

_____

_____

_____

```
P E A R S O N B E N S O N
E A D N A D E A U C H E I
T F G K C N W M O S S S D
T P Z G K A M T B V C Q A
Y R G A Y E A R B E O H L
J O H N S O N G U F T A L
I B W T X D C S M H T R E
R E N P Q B I G E M K V N
V R I B O C J D A T L I B
A T R V I C K E R S H C A
N S H E J Z T M S A U K C
S W A L T R I P V W X Y H
M A R L I N A L L I S O N
```

ALLISON
BENSON
BIGE
BUSCH
DALLENBACH
GANT
HARVIC
IRVAN
JOHNSON
KENSETH
MARLIN
MEARS
NADEAU
NEWMAN
PEARSON
PETTY
ROBERTS
SCOTT
VICKERS
WALTRIP

"He's the only kid I know who has sponsors for his trike."

©2004 Jonathan Ray Hawkins. Reprinted by permission.

SEASON WRAP-UP

The drivers in the Chase for the *NASCAR NEXTEL Cup* were:

Driver Name	Car #	Starting Position	Finishing Position
1. _____	_____	_____	_____
2. _____	_____	_____	_____
3. _____	_____	_____	_____
4. _____	_____	_____	_____
5. _____	_____	_____	_____
6. _____	_____	_____	_____
7. _____	_____	_____	_____
8. _____	_____	_____	_____
9. _____	_____	_____	_____
10. _____	_____	_____	_____

My driver was in the Chase: ❑ Yes ❑ No

My driver finished in _____ place with _____ points.

Drivers who finished 11 through 15 were:

11. _____, Car #_____

12. _____, Car #_____

13. _____, Car #_____

14. _____, Car #_____

15. _____, Car #_____

My favorite race of the whole season was: _____.

Because: _____

_____

NASCAR has something for everyone.

Wayne

NASCAR is, like, America.

Shelly

NASCAR races are as exciting as Christmas morning.

Nicole

NASCAR means staying up late!

Jason

My least favorite time of year is between the last NASCAR race and Speedweeks. I would rather clean my room then have no races on the weekends.

Seth

It's interesting—my dad likes country, my mom likes oldies like Madonna, my brother likes Rap, and I like Britney. But, we all love NASCAR!

Gail

NASCAR is . . .

_____

_____

_____

_____

_____

_____

_____

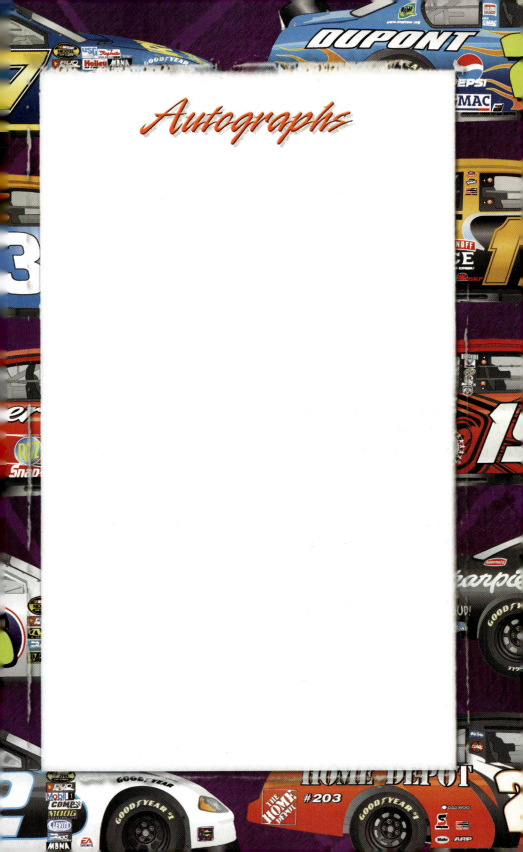

Autographs

Autographs

TRIVIA & WORD SCRAMBLE ANSWERS

NASCAR—Under the Hood

(Page 12)

1. **B**
2. **D**
3. **B**
4. **D**
5. **C**
6. **D**
7. **B**
8. **C**
9. **C**
10. **A**

Atlanta Motor Speedway

(Pages 17 & 18)

1. **B**
2. **D**
3. **D**
4. **D**
5. **C**
6. **A**
7. **A**
8. **C**
9. **D**
10. **B**

BUMP
ALLISON
PASSING
SCUFFS
RESTART

Bristol Motor Speedway

(Pages 25 & 26)

1. **C**
2. **B**
3. **D**
4. **A**
5. **D**
6. **B**
7. **D**
8. **D**
9. **C**
10. **D**

FRONTSTRETCH
WIN
DAYTONA
BACKSTRETCH
DARLINGTON

California Speedway

(Pages 31 & 32)

1. **C**
2. **A**
3. **C**
4. **A**
5. **B**
6. **C**
7. **A**
8. **C**
9. **B**
10. **A**

CAUTION
DODGE
JACKMAN
LEAD LAP
JOHNSON

Chicagoland Speedway

(Pages 37 & 38)

1. **D**	6. **D**
2. **D**	7. **A**
3. **D**	8. **B**
4. **D**	9. **C**
5. **C**	10. **B**

CARBURATOR
KENSETH
TELEMETRY
AIR DAM
SET UP

Daytona International Speedway

(Pages 49 & 50)

1. **A**	6. **C**
2. **A**	7. **D**
3. **C**	8. **A**
4. **D**	9. **D**
5. **B**	10. **A**

CHASSIS
QUALIFYING
CREW CHIEF
STOCK CAR
FABRICATOR

Darlington Raceway

(Pages 43 & 44)

1. **C**	6. **D**
2. **B**	7. **C**
3. **D**	8. **B**
4. **B**	9. **A**
5. **C**	10. **B**

ATLANTA
NASCAR
PIT
EARNHARDT
SPOTTER

Dover International Speedway

(Pages 57 & 58)

1. **C**	6. **D**
2. **C**	7. **C**
3. **B**	8. **B**
4. **A**	9. **C**
5. **B**	10. **D**

AERODYNAMICS
SPEED
INSPECTION
DRAFTING
PIT CREW

Homestead-Miami Speedway

(Pages 63 & 64)

1. **D**	6. **C**
2. **B**	7. **C**
3. **A**	8. **B**
4. **C**	9. **C**
5. **B**	10. **A**

WALL
GEARSHIFT
BLOCKING
GARAGE
GORDON

Infineon Raceway

(Pages 75 & 76)

1. **C**	6. **D**
2. **D**	7. **B**
3. **B**	8. **A**
4. **B**	9. **C**
5. **C**	10. **D**

TIRES
APPEARANCE
NEXTEL CUP
DRAG
JUNIOR

Indianapolis Motor Speedway

(Pages 69 & 70)

1. **C**	6. **B**
2. **A**	7. **D**
3. **C**	8. **C**
4. **D**	9. **D**
5. **B**	10. **C**

TEMPLATES
FLAGMAN
LOOSE
KAHNE
FUEL CELL

Kansas Speedway

(Pages 81 & 82)

1. **D**	6. **B**
2. **A**	7. **C**
3. **C**	8. **B**
4. **C**	9. **B**
5. **A**	10. **B**

CRASH
ENGINE
PIT ROAD
CHEVROLET
GREEN FLAG

Las Vegas Motor Speedway

(Pages 87 & 88)

1. **C**	6. **B**
2. **B**	7. **C**
3. **A**	8. **B**
4. **C**	9. **B**
5. **D**	10. **D**

MARLIN
POSITION
SPOILER
MECHANIC
TALLADEGA

Martinsville Speedway

(Pages 99 & 100)

1. **D**	6. **C**
2. **B**	7. **B**
3. **C**	8. **A**
4. **A**	9. **A**
5. **C**	10. **D**

HAULER
HELMET
FLAGS
SUSPENSION
HORSEPOWER

Lowe's Motor Speedway

(Pages 93 & 94)

1. **B**	6. **A**
2. **A**	7. **C**
3. **D**	8. **B**
4. **C**	9. **C**
5. **C**	10. **B**

GROOVE
CHAMPION
RACE TRACK
TIGHT
INDIANAPOLIS

Michigan International Speedway

(Pages 107 & 108)

1. **C**	6. **B**
2. **A**	7. **D**
3. **D**	8. **A**
4. **B**	9. **B**
5. **B**	10. **B**

POLE
SPONSOR
DRIVERS
PETTY
SUPERSPEEDWAY

New Hampshire International Speedway

(Page 113 & 114)

1. **B**		6. **B**	
2. **D**		7. **D**	
3. **A**		8. **A**	
4. **C**		9. **D**	
5. **C**		10. **A**	

FAN
CAMBER
WHEELBASE
VICKERS
DISPLACEMENT

Phoenix International Raceway

(Pages 121 & 122)

1. **D**		6. **B**	
2. **A**		7. **B**	
3. **A**		8. **A**	
4. **C**		9. **C**	
5. **C**		10. **B**	

NEWMAN
FRAME
TACHOMETER
RUBBER
SHOW CAR

Pocono Raceway

(Pages 127 & 128)

1. **C**		6. **D**	
2. **B**		7. **B**	
3. **D**		8. **C**	
4. **A**		9. **A**	
5. **A**		10. **B**	

AIR FLOW
SEVEN
FUEL MILEAGE
EXHAUST
STEERING

Richmond International Raceway

(Pages 135 & 136)

1. **D**		6. **A**	
2. **B**		7. **C**	
3. **C**		8. **B**	
4. **D**		9. **B**	
5. **A**		10. **C**	

RESTRICTOR PLATE
HARVICK
RPM
FORD
AUTOGRAPH

Talladega Superspeedway
(Pages 141 & 142)

1. **A**   6. **B**
2. **C**   7. **A**
3. **A**   8. **D**
4. **A**   9. **C**
5. **C**   10. **D**

CHECKERED FLAG
BANKING
WALTRIP
ROLL BAR
MC MURRAY

Watkins Glen International
(Pages 155 & 156)

1. **C**   6. **C**
2. **B**   7. **A**
3. **A**   8. **C**
4. **B**   9. **B**
5. **B**   10. **A**

BUSCH
BANKING
STEWART
HANDLING
ROOKIE

Texas Motor Speedway
(Pages 149 & 150)

1. **C**   6. **A**
2. **B**   7. **B**
3. **B**   8. **C**
4. **A**   9. **B**
5. **C**   10. **A**

SUNOCO
GASKET
PISTON
FOYT
INFIELD

Who is Jack Canfield,
Co-creator of *Chicken Soup for the Soul?*

Jack Canfield is one of America's leading experts in the development of human potential and personal effectiveness. He is both a dynamic, entertaining speaker and a highly sought-after trainer. Jack has a wonderful ability to inform and inspire audiences toward increased levels of self-esteem and peak performance. He has authored or co-authored numerous books including *Dare to Win, The Aladdin Factor, 100 Ways to Build Self-Concept in the Classroom, Heart at Work* and *The Power of Focus.* His latest book is *The Success Principles.*

www.jackcanfield.com

Who is Mark Victor Hansen,
Co-creator of *Chicken Soup for the Soul?*

In the area of human potential, no one is more respected than **Mark Victor Hansen**. For more than thirty years, Mark has focused solely on helping people from all walks of life reshape their personal vision of what's possible. His powerful message of possibility, opportunity and action have created powerful change in thousands of organizations and millions of individuals worldwide. He is a prolific writer of bestselling books such as *The One Minute Millionaire, The Power of Focus, The Aladdin Factor* and *Dare to Win.* His latest book is *Cracking the Wealth Code.*

www.markvictorhansen.com

Who is Matthew E. Adams

Matthew E. "Matt" Adams is a *New York Times* and *USA Today* best-selling coauthor of *Chicken Soup for the Soul of America, Chicken Soup for the NASCAR Soul,The Fast and Lean LOW CARB Racing Cookbook* and *Fairways of Life.* Matt can be seen regularly on *The Golf Channel* and *SpeedChannel.* He is also an accomplished public speaker. To book Matt for your next event, contact Jodi Syssa at IMG Speakers, *jsyssa@IMG WORLD.com* or (212) 774-6735. To send a message to Matt's office, e-mail him at *NASCARSoul@cox.net.*

Winning the Cup . . .

How sweet it is!